NEVER WORK FOR A JERK!

PATRICIA KING

NEVER WORK FOR A JERK!

A Dell Trade Paperback

Published by
Dell Publishing
a division of
The Bantam Doubleday Dell Publishing Group, Inc.
1 Dag Hammarskjold Plaza
New York, New York 10017

Grateful acknowledgment is made to the following for
permission to reprint published and copyrighted material:

Random House, Inc.: for opening quote to Chapter 2 from
The Corn Is Green by Emlyn Williams.

Alfred A. Knopf, Inc.: for the opening quote to Chapter 4
from *Something Happened* by Joseph Heller.

Richard Nelson: for the opening quote to Chapter 5 from
his adaptation of *The Marriage of Figaro* by Beaumarchais.

The Putnam Publishing Group: for the opening quote to
Chapter 6 from *The Once and Future King* by T. H. White.

Delacorte Press/Seymour Lawrence: for the opening quote
to Chapter 13 from *Galápagos* by Kurt Vonnegut.

Dell ® TM 681510, Dell Publishing Co., Inc.

ISBN: 0-440-50016-8

Reprinted by arrangement with Franklin Watts Inc.

Printed in the United States of America

April 1988

10 9 8 7 6 5 4 3 2 1

MV

THANK YOU TO

Brad Schwartz, who helped me
prepare this manuscript and
kept me sane, especially the day
the computer lost chapter thirteen.

Linda Perigo Moore, who encouraged
me by telling me when it was
right and helped me by telling me
what to do when it was wrong.
And who wrote the final sentence.

Al Zuckerman, who taught me
what this book should be.

Bill Newton, who believed in
this book from the beginning.

*Andy Puglise, Allan Ross, and
Doris Travis,*
who generously
contributed their ideas.

Kerry Ann King, darling daughter
and member of Team Xerox.

David Clark, who helps me believe
in myself by believing in me.

And
to the contributors of horror stories
who must remain nameless
lest their revelations haunt them.

To my father, Sam Puglise,
who taught me by his example
to take pride in my work and
do my best no matter who
I worked for or what I did.

CONTENTS

NEVER WORK FOR A JERK!

PREFACE

Years ago when management specialists in the United States were first getting interested in the "Japanese system of management," I worked in the management development department of a big New York City bank. My colleagues and I were offered an opportunity to see a film on Japanese management practices. We jumped at the chance. Going to the movies was a definite improvement over trying to get the reluctant managers of that organization to behave properly.

In the film, we saw a segment on how Japanese managers deal with frustration. One firm had constructed a special room, empty except for a padded column in the middle bearing the image of the company president; in one corner were a kid's baseball bat and a towel hanging from a hook.

A hidden camera recorded the following: A manager entered the room. He bowed to the image of the president, then removed his tie and jacket and hung them on the hook. He rolled up his sleeves, picked up the bat, and proceeded to beat the bejeezes out of the image in the center of the room. He hit it so hard and long that in the end he slumped over it in exhaustion. He put the bat back in the corner, mopped his face and neck with the towel, put on his tie and jacket, bowed again to the image, and left the room.

Wow. My colleagues and I were impressed. In our discussions that followed the film, we fantasized about having such a room at the bank. But we were sure that the image of the president wouldn't do. We had many demonic managers and supervisors whose images employees would prefer to batter. Why not, we decided, have pictures of all the bank's managers and supervisors printed on pillowcases and hung around the room. That way a disgruntled employee could enter the room, pick out the hated face, place the pillowcase over the padded column, and go ahead according to the Japanese procedure.

At this point it dawned on us what information we could collect from such a facility. All we would have to do is periodically inspect the pillowcases and fire the managers whose images showed the most wear. We had barely formulated this thought when we realized that those were precisely the people top management would probably want to promote. We went back to trying to teach the managers to behave better.

I have been at that game ever since—as a training manager at that bank and for the past fourteen years as a consultant to organizations from *Fortune* 500 companies to hospitals to owner-run mail order firms. I meet thousands of managers every year. A few are naturals; they know just how to create an atmosphere that fosters high productivity and creativity. Some improve a little with training; some even improve a lot. Most get no training. Many seem hopeless. Mostly, in programs designed to make them better managers, they complain about the people who manage them.

If you are a victim of bad management, you are not alone. Bad managers abound and the results of their mistakes are plain. Their employees trudge into the office or plant, leaking motivation. You can almost see it pouring out of their shoes as they leave their cars, trains, and buses and head for their work. Statistics on the low motivation of U.S. workers are grim. One study found that 75 percent admit not working up to their full potential. Half said they were doing only the minimum required. Sixty percent said they felt the trend was to do less and less.

Compare these numbers with companion statistics of employees' opinions of management. Less than a fourth of clerical employees feel they are being treated fairly. Less than two-fifths express confidence in the decisions made by top management. Half of clerical and hourly workers rate their companies only average or below. These data don't change much if you compare unionized or non-unionized workers.

These are the facts about workers at the lower echelons. You might think they'd improve if you asked the same questions of middle managers about *their* managers. Not a chance. Corporate executives are even more disillusioned. Less than 20 percent of them say they have great confidence in top management. Only a third rated American executives as "excellent" or "good." The parallels between effort expended by employees and their lack of respect for the folks at the top are no accident.

Bad management leads to employee listlessness which leads to loss of productivity. Instead of concentrating on producing results, a lot of us are conforming to useless rules, learning to be yes-men, and worrying about losing our jobs. Without clear leadership, we are spending too much time milling around or making false starts. In America today, pleasing the boss has become an end in itself and we do it even if we don't necessarily agree with or respect that boss. Some people seem to be spending most of their work time trying to guess what the boss wants and then doing it, regardless of how useless the activity.

Instead of producing results we're producing stress. We are suffering, getting sick. Many corporations respond to this by conducting programs in stress management for their employees. "Come to work for us," they say. "We'll put you to work in an impossible environment and we'll teach you yoga or exercise routines so you can deal with the stress."

Yoga and exercise are nice, and even beating the boss's image with a stick might help; but if you want to get rid of frustration, you have to go after its causes. If you think your boss or the management of your company is to blame, this book tells you what to do and why.

Basically, it tells you how to take charge of yourself, for yourself. The task is difficult but worth the risk. The stakes are high. Incompetent managers can make you sick. If the doctor mistreats you, you can sue. Some managers are so inept or wicked they create an environment that leads to heart attacks or nervous breakdowns. But you cannot sue your boss for malpractice. And complaining about a bad boss is hardly a substitute for job satisfaction. Your only defense is to get realistic about your expectations and learn to manage your relationship with your boss.

If you resent the notion that you should manage your boss, I don't blame you. You may say "the boss gets paid more, the boss should manage me." But this is Earth. All bosses are fallible; some are incompetent, or nasty. What are you going to do? Be resentful and wait for retirement? Be one of those dull, dependent people who went out of style with bell-bottoms? It's easy to be a victim or a loser. There are always drugs and alcohol to comfort you. It is easy to make the boss the ogre to blame for all your career frustrations. But the responsibility for building a good boss-employee relationship doesn't fall entirely on the boss. You are part of the equation. Besides, if your boss is comfortable with the status quo and you are uncomfortable, who is more likely to change? It is always the person who suffers from the situation who has to take the steps to change it. It is up to you to clarify the problems and seek solutions.

Taking action will make you feel better. You'll be an adult. You'll stop being a wimp and a complainer. You can stop getting hurt, taking on too much work, feeling like a dupe.

I'm not saying you're to blame for your boss's incompetence. But you are responsible for your own suffering if you sit around and take it. You may feel caged in, but the door is open.

Besides, if we all demand better management, they will have to give it to us. The passivity of employees has allowed organizations to get away with promoting twits and nitwits. If we won't stand for it anymore, they'll have to find us better leadership. And we'll all benefit.

Until those improvements arrive, you have to survive. Lots of people are badly managed and prosper anyway. Or they find ways of improving things. Or they get out. This book tells you how to analyze your situation, rectify it, or survive it until you take your chances with your next boss. Taking this advice requires a little spunk, but knowing your future is at stake, I'm sure you can master it.

By the way, a couple of matters of form. Bosses can be men or women. Rather than constantly use the phrases "he or she" and "him or her," I will use "he" sometimes and "she" sometimes. Also, the anecdotes in this book are based on the stories of real people I have met in my consulting career. Mostly, they are incidents I observed when I was called in to help ailing organizations. Sometimes they are the case histories of distressed people who came to me for advice. One or two describe the actions of managers who told me what they were doing but couldn't figure out why it wasn't working. I have changed the names of the people, the types of businesses they're in, and sometimes their sex to disguise their identities and avoid lawsuits. I hope, however, that the managers I describe here recognize themselves and see how destructive, stupid, and counterproductive they have been.

1

RATE YOUR BOSS QUIZ

*"The question is," said
Humpty Dumpty, "Which is
to be master—that's all."*

Lewis Carroll
*Alice's Adventures
in Wonderland*

You will probably want to read this whole book before you make any final decisions about your boss or your career. You need to examine your current position and your expectations and to base your action plan on a thorough analysis. But to get you started, here is a brief quiz. It will give you a general idea of where you stand with your boss.

Circle the number that applies and add up all the circled numbers to get your boss's score.

ALWAYS	ALMOST ALWAYS	SOMETIMES	ALMOST NEVER	NEVER		
4	3	2	1	0	1.	Does your boss make you feel important to him and the organization?
4	3	2	1	0	2.	Does your boss give you the credit and recognition you deserve?
4	3	2	1	0	3.	Does your boss give you challenging assignments and help you expand your capabilities?

4 3 2 1 0   4. Does your boss give you exposure to others, especially to her superiors?

4 3 2 1 0   5. Does your boss give clear directions as to what he wants done?

4 3 2 1 0   6. Does your boss set reasonable deadlines?

4 3 2 1 0   7. Does your boss avoid unnecessary changes in priorities?

4 3 2 1 0   8. Does your boss make you feel like an important part of the team?

4 3 2 1 0   9. Does your boss consider your point of view when she makes decisions that affect you?

4 3 2 1 0 10. Does your boss teach you things?

4 3 2 1 0 11. Does your boss encourage you to use your skills and creativity?

4 3 2 1 0 12. Does your boss tell you the truth about your work even if it is unpleasant?

4 3 2 1 0 13. Does your boss avoid unnecessary political power games?

4 3 2 1 0   14. Does your boss help you see how your goals mesh with the organization's goals?

4 3 2 1 0   15. Is your boss committed to what he does?

4 3 2 1 0   16. Is your boss fair in making decisions about salary, promotions, and bonuses?

4 3 2 1 0   17. Does your boss avoid win-lose battles with you?

4 3 2 1 0   18. Can you tolerate your boss's flaws?

4 3 2 1 0   19. Does your boss solve problems well? Does she adapt well to different situations?

4 3 2 1 0   20. Is your boss organized? Does he spend time on important work and avoid trivia?

4 3 2 1 0   21. Is your boss confident in herself?

4 3 2 1 0   22. Does your boss empathize with your position when something goes wrong? Can you turn to him for support?

4 3 2 1 0   23. Does your boss let you in on things?

4 3 2 1 0   24. Does your boss listen well?

4 3 2 1 0   25. Does your boss give you authority to match your responsibility and make sure you have what you need to get the job done?

4 3 2 1 0   26. Does your boss handle conflict well?

4 3 2 1 0   27. Does your boss praise your good work more than she criticizes your mistakes?

4 3 2 1 0   28. Does your boss communicate clearly?

4 3 2 1 0   29. Does your boss learn from his own mistakes?

4 3 2 1 0   30. Can your boss get tough when it's really necessary?

Add up the boss's ratings and test the boss against this measure:

Score   *Conclusion*

120–91   You have a good, maybe even a great boss. Stick with this person; learn all you can. Read this book to find out how to make the most of your advantageous position.

90–51	There's real hope. You can probably learn to work comfortably with this boss. Start taking an active role in your own supervision. Follow the advice in this book to rectify the problems and capitalize on the boss's strengths.
50–26	Don't be too optimistic. Make an attempt to improve things, but unless this boss is very new in the job, start thinking about your next move. Read chapter fifteen first; then read other chapters for advice on how to cope.
25–0	Your boss is a terminal jerk. Get out fast. Stop reading this book for now and start writing your resume. Depending on the state of your health and your pocketbook, it might be wise to resign immediately. Read this book for advice on how to cope in the meantime or how to choose better next time.
Caveat:	Perhaps your boss scores high and you still hate him. If you have trouble getting along with any boss, you may want to read chapter 14 before you read the rest of this book.

2

TAKE
CHARGE

*We all walk in the dark,
Morgan, and each of us
must turn on his own light.*

Emlyn Williams
The Corn Is Green

Good management is worth searching out or fighting for. Under effective leaders, you can feel significant. You will learn. You will derive satisfaction from and take pride in your competence and achievements. You will have a sense of community with your coworkers. Work will excite you. Your motivation will flow and your productivity will increase.

Bad management destroys these satisfactions. It can poison your character. You will find yourself accommodating to the status quo. You will learn to give as good as you get. By knuckling under, you will become one of them.

By learning to manage your boss or taking the trouble to find a good boss, you can earn more job satisfaction, bring more motivation to the job, and likely make more money and have more fun.

To do this your relationship with your boss must meet your needs. You and he must work together in a way that complements both your styles. In an atmosphere of mutual respect, you should be able to communicate clearly your expectations of one another. You need to be able to trust one another and to be honest with one another.

Both of you need to feel powerful. A healthy boss-subordinate relationship means you realize you depend on one another to meet your own goals. You learn to draw on one another's strengths. This means more than just satisfying one another's neuroses. It means knowing and respecting one another's abilities and compensating for one another's weaknesses. It also means that both of you are willing to listen and to speak your minds.

That may sound like heaven, but you can approach this ideal if you are willing to act. Otherwise what can you do? Being good and keeping your nose clean are not the answer.

That's a lesson Marlene Miranda learned early in her career. Now she's the administrative assistant to the chairman of the board of a major magazine publisher. She loves her job and is highly respected in her firm and by her friends. But she still remembers her difficulties with her first boss. After high school and one year of secretarial school, she went to work in the treasurer's department of a large, packaged-goods company. Her boss was a slave driver and an eccentric, but Marlene didn't question his actions. She had no basis of comparison, so she thought it was normal when he gave her rush tasks at 4:30 that kept her until 6:30 or 7:00 at night. He called her at home to dictate reports over the phone so she could go in early the next morning to type them. Some of her friends made fun of her for being too compliant, but she liked to think of herself as performing above and beyond the call of duty. She was an adult, doing adult things; and because she was still living with her parents, she thought the urgent late night and early morning phone calls from the boss made her look important at home. She sometimes felt her boss was taking advantage of her good nature, but she didn't complain. She knew that if she just worked hard and did a good job she would be rewarded.

One winter night she didn't leave the office until nearly ten o'clock. She was driving her usual route along the back roads from her suburban office building to her parents' home. It was cloudy and the roads were very dark. When Marlene first suspected that another car was following hers, she told herself not to be silly, that it was probably her imagination. But she made sure her doors were locked anyway, and she watched carefully. Whenever she turned, the car behind her turned, too. Before long, no matter how she fought the thought, she became convinced she was being followed. Since the roads were windy and damp from rain earlier in the day, Marlene was reluctant to speed up to get away from her pursuer. As she came to a straight section of road, she started to accelerate when the car behind her overtook her and forced her off the road. Her heart pounded and her mind raced as she watched a man get out of the other car and approach her. Then she recognized the man as her boss. When she rolled down her window, he looked her in the eye and said, "Take a letter."

Today Marlene confesses that she actually fumbled in the glove compartment, found a pad and pencil, and took a letter. "I don't know why I did it," she says. "I should have run him over instead."

Marlene's story may sound preposterous but she says it's true and I believe her. You may think no sane person would take dictation from such a brute. It is easy to judge Marlene, to call her overly submissive, to imagine that most people would have flatly refused to comply. Perhaps Marlene is unusual because she did what she was told in such extreme circumstances. But employees are often inordinately obedient.

WHY ARE WE
SO COMPLIANT?

In the first place, we start out assuming that organizations are rational places. We think the people in authority are smarter and understand the big picture better than we do. We figure their decisions, no matter how demented they sound, must be based on superior knowledge. Eventually we learn that we work in complex and sometimes chaotic places where unreasonable decisions are as easy to make as sane ones, and where the people in charge do not necessarily have the skill or intelligence a good manager needs. We come to understand this only after years of disappointments. It takes us a while to wise up because the prevailing culture militates against our reaching these conclusions and acting on them. It does this in several ways.

Respect for authority has been strongly valued in our families and schools. Even parents who want to raise their children to think independently find it hard to put up with offspring who question authority. Most of us have been forced to accept "because I say so" as a rationale from teachers and parents. This authoritarianism makes us passive. Some of us are so indoctrinated that we have convinced ourselves that we prefer this. Of course, we need to have an orderly society. There are too many of us on this planet for each of us to go his own way. We must avoid chaos. But that doesn't mean we have to follow along like mindless boobs. That won't help.

Good manners in our society also dictate that we be nice and pleasant. This is a strong value. I have been in organizations where it is all right to be inhuman as long as you are pleasant, but it's a sin to be human if it means being unpleasant. Collaboration, cooperation, and trust are wonderful values and necessary for a peaceful and productive society, but in some places anyone who has a mind of his own is criticized for not being a "team player."

In the fear-ridden atmosphere prevalent in so many of today's organizations, people will waste time, effort, money—anything to avoid conflict. If someone has a numbskull idea for moving the engineering department to Beverly Hills, in many corporations you express your astonishment and dismay by saying, "I have a concern about your idea, Hal."

We need to learn to be more forceful. Without destroying, we need to shake things up. Without being insubordinate, we need to question decisions that affect our lives. Without injuring, we need to express our dissension clearly.

CORPORATE NEWSPEAK LEADS TO CORPORATE NOTHINK

In modern corporations, hardly anybody has the guts to speak directly. Managers make vague suggestions, and in their desire to please, employees interpret the suggestions as directives. In one of the world's largest banks, the general auditor once remarked at a meeting, "It would be interesting to know how people learn to breach computer security." His assistant manager formed a task force to study the question. Two months later a thirty-page report that the general auditor really didn't want appeared on his desk. Later we found that all six people who worked on that report thought it an asinine idea to waste two months studying a moot question. But they were all good corporate citizens; none of them disagreed openly. One said she discussed the insanity of the project over lunch with a colleague, but neither of them had mentioned the problem to the assistant manager. Eventually, when the general auditor received the report, he was shocked at the time and effort that went into complying with a request he never intended to make. What he had expressed as idle curiosity his assistant manager had taken for a work assignment.

Why didn't anyone complain? Why didn't one

person fight back? Why do people act dumb when they're not? Why do we all put up with tyrants, dunces, and incompetents? Our traditional values and our current mores make us pliable, but our heritage also teaches us to reject waste, stupidity, and domination. Despite this, in the daily working out of things, people often do what they are told regardless of how muddleheaded it is. They are frightened by people they think are more articulate or aggressive or influential. Everyone seems to be afraid of something—losing the job, making a bad impression, damaging career potential, not getting a raise. They feel impotent so they accept bad management.

THIS POWERLESSNESS
IS A MIRAGE

The feeling is real, but it isn't based on reality. We endow our bosses with the power they have over us. We do this by deciding to work for them. We do this by needing their approval. We do it by cooperating with them. Our own feelings of guilt may make resisting difficult, but we could, if we wanted to, question the daffier assignments, articulate our needs, and demand the respect we deserve. Many of us could influence things for the better just by speaking up.

But speaking up takes courage. Where do you get courage? That's hard to say, but you may find yours by thinking about a few things. First of all, understand that your own happiness and well-

being are at stake. Research shows that job satisfaction is second only to love as a predictor of a
person's happiness. Your boss has a great influence on your job satisfaction. The steps you take
to improve the way you are managed are part of
your personal pursuit of happiness.

EVALUATE YOUR SITUATION
AND TAKE ACTION

If you have been afraid to talk to your boss, figure
out if your fears are well-founded. Make sure your
expectations are realistic. If you have been calling
your boss a jerk, have the guts to ask yourself if
the label fits. If you go around blaming boss after
boss or the organization, you may be scapegoat-
ing them for problems that are inside you. Some
people feel imprisoned in their jobs and get new
jobs only to find out that the bars on the windows
move with them. Part of the problem may be you.

Realize, also, that regardless of where the difficulty is, you are the one who will have to take
the action. Be careful of waiting, of living on the
fantasy that top management will reorganize the
department and give you a better boss. Or that a
safe will fall on the rascal's head. Justice seldom
happens by accident. Once in a while, top management owns up to its mistakes and puts things
right. But don't count on it. If you are being victimized by a dastardly taskmaster, you are going
to have to stage your own heroic rescue. Robin
Hood and Indiana Jones are busy elsewhere. Blow

your own trumpets, break your own psychological bonds, cheer your own victory.

But watch out for grandstand plays. If you start loud fights with your boss, you may get a reputation as a malcontent. Even if your boss gets the heave-ho, you may find he'll be holding the door open for you as you follow him out.

Besides, fighting can be harder on you than it is on the boss. She may walk around feeling self-righteous while you seethe. She may remain calm and in control, while your blood pressure goes wild.

While you are dealing with the problem, try to see it as a learning experience. This will be hard. Whenever I tell him my troubles, my dad has a habit of saying adversity is good for my character. I always used to say that I didn't think there was that much wrong with my character as it was. Finally I realized that even if you don't think your character needs it, it is best to see your troubles as a way of improving yourself. It helps you get through the day.

If others observe you when you are in difficulty, showing that you know how to behave can boost your career. It's tricky to show you are patient and courageous at the same time. Striking a balance between being a hothead or a wimp may tax you, but others will make conclusions about your judgment based on how you act when you're up against a difficult manager. The pragmatic approach is to use the catastrophe to your own advantage, to show you can handle it.

FIGURE OUT WHAT
IS RIGHT FOR YOU
AND JUST DO IT

Sometimes this means taking a risk and jumping with both feet. That's what Eve Kimble had to do. She was working for a placement firm, a small company owned by a megalomaniac named Charlie Ralston. Although Charlie profited financially from her successes, his ego suffered in the face of her accomplishments. He wanted to be the only star in the show. He assigned her the most difficult tasks. If she failed at them, he rubbed salt in her wounds. If she succeeded, he found ways to criticize her personal style and show her how she had succeeded despite her shortcomings. He had a favorite ruthless game. He would present her with what he called a challenge—a problem to solve. But he would hold back some of the information she needed to get the right answer. He would make fun of her attempts to solve it. Then, when she ran out of ideas, he would show her how easy it was for him to come up with the right answer.

Charlie's strikes went right for Eve's psychological jugular. She was a sucker for the word "challenge." It made her determined to succeed, to prove her capabilities. After a while, her confidence ebbed. Bright and competent as she was, she began to feel inadequate. She questioned whether she should leave her job, but she was a committed, dedicated person. She began to see winning over Charlie as the ultimate challenge. She stayed.

Then she started losing things, forgetting things, having headaches. One day she forgot where she put her car in a multilevel parking garage. She wandered around looking for it. Soon she noticed that someone was following her. The thief stole her purse at gunpoint.

Charlie didn't mug Eve, but he did bring out the victim in her. He did confuse her about her competence to the point where she became confused about everything. After the mugging, she began to see what a victim she had become. She became more afraid of staying than she was of leaving. She talked it over with a friend at lunch one day. They decided there was only one solution to her problem. Eve went back to her desk that afternoon, collected her belongings and walked out. She saw, perhaps rightly so, that getting out of that environment was tantamount to saving her life.

It took courage for Eve to quit her job before she had another one. But she did what she had to do. Bruce Addison, on the other hand, needed patience to cope with his situation. He worked for the continuing education department of a university. He had had a long, happy relationship with Art, his manager. They thought alike about many things. Bruce was learning and growing and content for nearly three years. Then the climate changed. The school's political situation heated up, budgets were being cut, and Art was suddenly under great pressure. His behavior became bizarre—he asked Bruce to take on clerical tasks that Bruce resented. He started going over Bruce's expenses and wrongfully accusing him of cheating. He often went out abruptly, leaving Bruce to make lame excuses to people who called. He suddenly had total recall of Bruce's mistakes and amnesia when it came to Bruce's accomplishments. He gave Bruce derogatory performance appraisals and showed him in his worst light to university administration. Bruce wrote his resume and started looking for a new job. Although the process was slow, he decided to stick it out where he was until he found another job.

One day, though, he reached his wits' end after Art bawled him out in front of some students. Bruce called up a friend and complained that he felt trapped. "I can't stand this; I'm a prisoner here. I'm going nuts," he said. "You're free," his friend told him. "You could get up, pick up your car keys, say a couple of choice words to Art, walk out to the parking lot, and drive away. No one would send the police after you. You are still there because you decided to stick it out until you find another job. You can change your mind, but if you stay, remember you are doing it because you want to for now." It helped Bruce to remember that he stayed there of his own free will because it served his purposes. Knowing that he could walk out helped him cope with an otherwise intolerable situation. Sticking it out, being patient, did not make Bruce a coward. It made him a man who knew what he needed to do and did it.

YOU HAVE THREE CHOICES

If you have a bad boss, you can try to improve the way you're managed, you can grin and bear it, or you can get another job. Of the three, grinning and bearing it is my least favorite. First of all, few people grin while they're bearing it. They moan and groan. They make themselves sick, and they drive their friends and families nuts with their complaints. If you are going to grin and bear it, you have to accept the situation and make your peace with it. Quit the chronic complaining. Remember, martyrs are loved and admired only after they're dead.

I also dislike the grin-and-bear-it approach because it means that bad bosses stay where they are and that employees compensate for *the boss's* shortcomings. Top management never sees the pain caused by its poor choices. No one links the loss of morale and productivity to the behavior of inept managers and supervisors. This perpetuates the problem. Top management continues to make the same mistakes and the wrong people continue to be promoted. Some places seem to have a personnel policy that excludes everyone but incompetents and mediocrities from becoming bosses. An overabundance of employee patience with bad management also means that insufferable managers will see no reason or way to improve.

Sometimes, though, one has no choice. Walt and Allen Scavone work for their father. They will inherit the business from him. He may be a tyrant, but it's worth it to them to hang on. Sondra

Basler works in the only bank in her small town. Getting another job in town would mean taking a cut in pay or status. Getting a job in another bank would mean commuting for more than an hour each way and not spending much time with her kids. Sondra is staying in her job even though, to hear her describe it, her boss is possessed by the ghost of Attila the Hun.

SIZE UP YOUR SITUATION

One possible course of action is to change your relationship with your boss. I said change the relationship; I most emphatically did not say change the boss. If you think you are going to change your boss's personality, give up now. Twelve years of psychotherapy with a trained analyst isn't guaranteed to change a person's basic personality. And psychotherapists have the advantage of working with people who want to change. It's unlikely that anything you will do can make a dent in what kind of person your boss is.

On the other hand, you may have a good chance of changing the way you and the boss relate to one another. Start by trying to understand yourself and the boss better. Think about your strengths and weaknesses. Compare the way you like to work with his style of management. Think about your own goals and your boss's goals and what each of you is doing to achieve them. Any comfortable boss-subordinate relationship is going to be based on helping one another realize these goals, by concentrating on one another's assets, and by working out a mutually acceptable style of interacting.

If you have been having problems, figure out where they come from. What is it in your behavior or the boss's behavior that is causing the friction? Learn how you get on one another's nerves and try to change those behaviors.

In the story about Bruce, there was a clue to why Art behaved as he did. Budget pressures or pressures from the top were causing Art his own troubles. True, Art had no right to take his problems out on Bruce. Knowing why Art acts as he does doesn't make his behavior right, but it does make it understandable. Your boss may bark at you because he is tactless or she may make bad decisions because she's a moron. Once you toss the boss into one of those categories, however, you arrive at a dead end. Well, maybe not a dead end. There is one exit. But only one. You have to quit.

Instead of just stereotyping your boss, find a productive way to analyze the problem. Figure out how your boss likes to work, how he likes to communicate, what his pet peeves are. Adapting a bit can make all the difference. Two people stranded on two different desert islands each had an alarm clock. One threw the clock in the ocean, thinking he had no use for something to wake him up in the morning. The other took the clock apart and made the insides into fishing hooks. Survival often depends on the ability to adapt. Understanding the pressures on your boss will make it easier for you to adapt. Your empathy may motivate you to bend a little in her direction, to solve the conflicts between you, to make the relationship more satisfying for both of you. The next two chapters will help you analyze what you can rightfully and reasonably expect from your boss and how to communicate your needs productively. They will help you decide on a course of action and carry it out.

Life at work need not be grim if you use your wits to make your work-life rewarding. If things are horrid for you now, fix them. If you can't redeem your situation, get out.

3

WHAT CAN YOU REASONABLY EXPECT?

Perfection is such a nuisance.

Emile Zola

I once asked a room full of managers to define a good boss. They got together in small groups and reinvented the Boy Scout oath. Their list of adjectives even included "good-looking." The boss they wanted would be the perfect candidate for canonization. That's the problem with abstract thinking about what makes for a good boss. Inside us lives that little person who wants perfection. The perfect parent, the perfect spouse, the perfect child, the perfect boss. That way lies frustration. And conflict. And failure.

Step one in getting along with your boss is to be realistic in evaluating what makes a good manager. You'll have trouble if you try to do this in the abstract. Instead you need to determine what is most important to you. Here are some things to think about as you size up your manager and your job.

YOUR NEEDS MAKE THE DIFFERENCE

If you are old enough to work, you must have your own idiosyncrasies, your own pet peeves, and your own special needs. These will influence what you most need in a boss. Perhaps your boss is wonderful at all the other management behaviors but doesn't remember to praise people for their good work. If you are one of those people who needs a good deal of reassurance, it is unlikely that the boss's other good qualities will compensate you for the lack of what you need most from a boss. You need to match your needs to your manager's strengths. You can do this by getting your boss to do the thing that you most need done, or by finding a boss who readily displays the behaviors most important to you.

To make this match, you need to assess your needs. Be as honest with yourself as you can. On your own or with someone to help, figure out: What are your strengths and weaknesses? How dependent are you on authority figures? What style of working with a boss is most comfortable for you? With this information you can try to mesh your own style with that of your boss. At the very least you will understand, when the relationship goes wrong, why you feel as frustrated as you do. It will allow you to analyze the situation a little more dispassionately. You may be able to see any conflict between you and your boss as a result of incompatibilities within both of you, instead of seeing her as the entire cause of the problem.

This analysis may also enable you to accommodate to your boss's style. If you like to make decisions about your work on your own and then pass them by the boss for approval, you may balk if your boss prefers to discuss things thoroughly before deciding. But maybe you can convert to the boss's way of thinking without feeling as if you've given up something vital about yourself. Some accommodations could do violence to your individuality, but others will be minor or even temporary adjustments. Besides, you will feel better if *you* have decided to include the boss, rather than having the boss butt in.

You come to the job not just with your hands and your head; your guts come with you. You bring your needs as a human being to the office, plant, or shop. You need a situation that satisfies as many of those human needs as possible. You want your boss to give you work and pay. If you are ambitious, you also want raises and promotions. You may look for friendship, approval, and esteem. You may not be happy in your work unless it gives you a challenge, an opportunity to stretch your skills and knowledge to capacity.

Few people feel content with their jobs if they have bad relations with the person in charge; our feelings about work-life are colored by how we feel about the boss. Bosses are seldom neutral in how they affect our deepest human feelings—the need for financial and physical security, recognition, control over decisions that affect our lives, and a sense of belonging. Regardless of your other satisfactions in life, you are likely to feel disgruntled at work if your boss's style is totally out of sync with your needs—if your boss gives you what you don't need and doesn't give you what you do need.

BOSSES CREATE
OR ALLEVIATE STRESS

If the boss is unbearable, work becomes a source of stress instead of a source of satisfaction. These days stress is public enemy number one. We read and hear frequent reports of how it contributes to disease. Living in today's society creates more than enough strain; you certainly don't want a boss who creates more just because she has the opportunity.

But not all stress is bad. Some things should tense you up. Anxiety is what keeps you from walking in front of a truck. And having a few problems to solve can get your creative juices flowing. One of the worst work environments I've ever seen was an advertising agency where being pleasant was the number one criterion for getting ahead. No one was ever negative, at least not publicly. The employees were so fearful of being harsh with one another that they barely communicated. But in private, the people in the media department complained to one another about the shoddy treatment they received from the people in account management. The account execs made jokes among themselves about the people in the creative department. The creatives called everyone else in the agency "the suits" and did their best to ignore them. Apparently oblivious to all the animosity beneath the surface, the top management prided itself on the pleasant atmosphere. They used the term "family" to describe the agency. Depending on whose family you compared it to, I guess they could have been right. There were no shouting matches. There wasn't much visible dissension. But there weren't any award-winning advertising ideas, either. Real cooperation interrupted by occasional passionate outbursts would have fostered more creativity than that superficial, make-nice environment.

Some stress is important; too much is deadly. The job and the boss can cause you to overdose on stress in a lot of different ways: by giving you too much to do, by making you insecure about keeping your job, by constantly changing or keeping secret the criteria by which you are judged, by giving you inadequate equipment or responsibility without authority, by involving you in personal conflicts, boring work, or noxious working conditions. Your boss plays an important role in creating or alleviating these forms of stress.

The symptoms and results of too much stress are well-known: loss of sleep or appetite, headache, backache, skin rashes, depression, pain in the neck and shoulders, and menstrual irregularity. Severe or chronic stress can cause ulcers, asthma, colitis, hypertension, heart disease, and mental breakdowns. Resistance to stress is part of your body's resistance to disease. If you feel compelled to do something about stress on the job, that's a healthy sign that your body and mind are trying to keep you sane and whole.

Experts feel that your family cannot compensate you for having an unbearable boss. Sure they can love you and shore up your battered self-esteem, but they cannot stop you from feeling stress on the job, where it does damage to your body that cannot be repaired at home. In fact, many people bring home the tension from their work problems and end up spoiling their family relationships.

A good boss can make it easy for you to deal with stress on the job. Studies show that regardless of how difficult work conditions seem, people who feel they have the support of their bosses file half as many medical claims as those whose bosses don't support them. In another study, researchers found that people with bad bosses had higher blood serum cholesterol. In this latter case the bad bosses were defined as being too bossy, sticklers for rules, and unwilling or unable to help employees see the larger picture.

But we can't define a good boss just as someone who doesn't give you a heart attack. Let's look at the positive side. The best bosses teach you how to succeed. They use their power to help you grow. They influence you for the good—your good. Grown-ups don't need parents and good bosses are careful not to overemphasize this role. Some people resent being "parented." But most of us want support and encouragement to help us develop.

HOW DO YOU RECOGNIZE A GOOD BOSS?

You really can't recognize good managers by looks—they can be fat or thin, male or female, tall or short, black or white. You can, however, recognize them by their actions. What they do and what they don't do is what counts. Personalities are likely to enter into it, but a good boss doesn't have to be likable. And some of the worst are very likable. Warmth is a rotten quality in an inept boss. It makes you stick around longer than you should. You feel guilty saying anything against sweet old Elmer even though he makes stupid decisions and refuses to fight your battles for you when you need him.

Behavior is the key. You want a boss who helps you feel effective and powerful, not one who wants to feel this way at your expense. You want someone who gives you the knowledge and helps you develop the skills you need to do things yourself, not one who does things for you.

Good managers are not always great leaders. Leaders need vision and a capacity to communicate that vision; they must be single-minded in their quest of their goals. Good managers, on the other hand, may be good administrators who just do what needs to be done to help their people get the work out and feel good about it. Dave Stanislovsky, for instance, runs the mail room at a telephone company. He's done that for eight years and he'll probably do it for another eight until he retires. He's never been a candidate for higher management and that seems just fine with him. No one would ever call Dave a charismatic leader. But as far as I'm concerned, he could give management lessons to some of the hotshots in the company who understand little about human motivation.

Dave is a patient teacher. He makes sure the people who work for him understand exactly what's required of them. He demands excellent work, but he shows his appreciation for it. His vision is a narrow one. He wants work materials and mail to move efficiently and accurately around the building. But he is dedicated to his goal and the strength of his commitment makes it contagious.

The people who work for him understand the importance of their work.

Nor is Dave super-serious. He's the cartoon king of the company. He slips jokes clipped from newspapers and magazines into the mail deliveries. The legal department gets the ones about lawyers, the computer people the ones about computers, and so on. He loves telling people jokes and laughs loudest when someone plays a little trick on him. But the jokes and the laughs never get in the way of the work.

Over the years Dave has instituted several cost-saving ideas. Many excellent employees began working for Dave and moved on into higher paid jobs. They always remember him as someone who got them off to a good start. He has been a mainstay in the company's efforts to employ the mentally handicapped.

Dave is not a flashy or riveting individual. He's a steady, reliable manager whose people get a great deal of satisfaction out of doing their jobs well.

Dave's experience shows that a good boss doesn't have to be a genius. He does, however, have to be able to think things out and solve problems. Knowledge is another requisite. A good boss doesn't necessarily know more about your job than you do. If you know more, a good boss will respect that superior knowledge and will seek your advice. But he must know enough to distinguish poor from good from superior work. It helps if he also understands how much effort the work requires.

Good managers show their enthusiasm by their focus on the work. The intensity of their feelings about the work attracts us to it and to them. They also have a way of making the abstract tangible, of helping us visualize a future for ourselves or a result of our work that takes on a reality all its own. That vision brings out our motivation and commitment.

If you want to see the results of good management, watch the commitment and energy levels of people. You can do this anywhere—in a restaurant, a bank, your office or plant. People who believe in their managers go about their business wholeheartedly. If they are led by people they trust, they aren't distracted by external matters. Take the contrast I saw in two chemical companies.

One, a giant with a name everyone knows, is managed by people who look only at numbers and make decisions without regard to the needs of the people in the organization, the quality of its products, or its viability over the long haul. Process engineers are judged only on how much they can shave off in production costs often at the expense of product quality or worker safety. The training department is judged by how many people attend how many training programs in a year, without any attempt made to measure what the people are learning or how the training affects their job performance. You can find pockets of good management in this company, but they are miraculous little exceptions to the general rule of management by cutting corners. The dominant management style is to put things before people—before employees, before customers, before the rest of the human race that inhabits this increasingly polluted planet.

The general atmosphere is one of depression. People go to work without enthusiasm. The most energetic moment of the day comes at 4:22. That's the earliest people can walk out without causing an eyebrow to raise. They jump; the energy in their voices increases. There's a bounce in their steps as they walk toward the parking lot, a zip to their stride that is entirely missing during the day.

In a slightly smaller, competitive company, people trust their managers to make concerned decisions. Employees come to work with energy and enthusiasm. They are serious about business but they are clearly enjoying themselves. Employees often tell the story of how their company pulled a product off the market because they had data to show it might be carcinogenic. "The product met government standards," they will tell you, "but we weren't sure so we pulled it." It cost the company profits and them their bonuses, but they are proud because the company did the right thing. When they face problems, they experience the same difficulties that their counterparts in the other company do, but they tackle them with energy. People enjoy going home to their families, but they also enjoy coming to work. They are managed well and they show it.

Well-managed people are not necessarily free of stress. Good bosses aren't always happy and painless to have around. Sometimes a boss can cause employees stress or even make them unhappy just by doing a good job. If a person doesn't perform up to standard and a talented manager has tried all the right ways to get that person to

shape up, she may have to fire the poor per-
former. That doesn't make her a bad boss. In fact,
it may prove that she really cares about the productivity of the group and about the morale of the
people who have to take up the slack for the slug-
gard.

In essence, good managers see employees as
competent and creative. They know that employees have their own goals that create within them
the motivation needed to produce goods or services of high quality. Good bosses tap into that
energy. Unfortunately, studies show that four out
of five managers see their subordinates as lazy and
not very smart. They act from a fundamental be-
lief that people are motivated by fear or money
and by little else. Noel Boardman was one such
manager. His basic premise was that everyone was
trying to take advantage of him and the car rental
company where he ran the advertising department. He believed his people would give him a
good day's work only if he forced them to do so.

When Susan Markham came to work for him
he knew she had knowledge and skill. She had
been an account executive in a major advertising
agency and her previous boss had given her a
glowing recommendation. During her interview,
he talked only about the job and what it required.
She expressed enthusiasm for the demanding work
he described. He assumed she said she liked to
work hard because she wanted the job. In his mind,
applicants would say anything to impress a pro-
spective boss. But he hired Susan anyway because
she was smart and seemed compliant.

During her first two months on the job, he watched Susan very carefully. He told her exactly what he wanted her to do and she did it. She came in early and stayed late. He figured he had a winner. But then he started to see signs that made him suspicious.

Susan came to him and said, "I've been on the job long enough now to feel comfortable with the work. I've got a few ideas I'd like to suggest." That in itself was not a problem. But the suggestions she made all had to do with what she called productivity and what he saw as a way of getting out of work. He rejected most of her proposals and told her that their methods were "tried and true." She seemed disappointed but he thought, *Tough. This isn't a country club, and she gets paid more than twice as much as I got when I was her age.*

In the months that followed he noticed that Susan wasn't working as hard as she had in the past. Sometimes she came in a little after nine. On several days, he saw her leave exactly at five. *It's time, he thought, to put on the screws.*

He called her in and told her he felt her work was falling off. He gave her a couple of special assignments; he set the closest possible due dates. When she objected that these new projects would interfere with her regular work, he was sure she was a slacker like the rest of the people he had hired from ad agencies. *They're all alike, he thought. They want to be big shots without working.*

From Noel's perspective, Susan resisted his attempts to get her to work hard. Eventually, just before he was about to give her a bad performance appraisal and a warning about her future with the company, she left. "She saw the handwriting on the wall. She knew she wasn't going to get away with doing nothing," he told me.

I suggested that she might have been sincere in her desire to improve her performance, that perhaps her motivation had been eroded when her ideas were rejected. Noel looked at me with the pity he reserved for the truly naive. "You'll learn the hard way, the way I did," he told me. "People aren't as good as you'd like to believe they are."

A good boss gets high productivity from people by inspiring them to work hard. Bad bosses try to blackmail or bribe productivity out of people. It works for a while and then, like Noel's pressure tactics, it backfires.

Good bosses need to have confidence in their people, but they also need confidence in themselves. Confident managers don't have to play ego games with their subordinates. They don't have to prove they're right all the time. They can empathize and work as "first among equals" to find solutions to problems or plans of action.

If your boss is a good boss, she will do many things to help you, herself, and the organization to succeed. First of all, she will help you focus on your strengths and capabilities and how you can use those talents to further the company's goals, gain satisfaction from the contribution you are making, and help you learn and grow in ways that are important to you. In other words, she will help you, within the scope of the job, become an effective person, in your own eyes and in the eyes of others.

Flexibility is also a hallmark of a good boss. If your boss has to have everything done his way, if he doesn't allow you to use your own ideas, your creativity can dry up. It also helps if your boss knows how to set priorities and keep things moving.

A good boss will concentrate on good communication. He will give clear instructions, take the time to make sure you understand priorities, encourage you, and help you solve problems as the work progresses.

Good bosses listen.

Good bosses reward performance. They notice when you've done something admirable and admire it. They give you more than just the famous "Attaboy." They say specifically what you did to deserve their admiration, why they think it was difficult to do what you did, and why it's valuable to the organization. They also do their best to get you the raises and promotions you deserve.

All this is not to say that good bosses are warm, fuzzy Father Gepettos who are always nice. They maintain discipline, make the tough, sometimes unpopular decisions, and do what needs to be done to make the group a success.

Good bosses let you in on what's going on in the organization. They are generous with inside information. Unlike their insecure counterparts, they see information as something to be shared, not something to be hoarded and used as a source of power.

Good bosses are available. They spend time with their people. They are there to give advice and encouragement, clear an obstacle, and cheer a good halftime score.

Please notice that what we have been talking about here is the boss's behavior. These are not personality traits. Good bosses have all kinds of personalities. What is important is that they do most of these things and do them consistently. Your boss may not have to do all of them to please you.

Ideally, you and the boss will learn to accommodate each other and to work as a team in a way that satisfies both of you. If you understand one another's needs, you can disagree without being disagreeable. You will understand one another even when you don't agree.

A wonderful boss can inspire you. I've worked with a couple of people who have changed my life. They had an image of me and my potential before I had developed the confidence to tap my own talents. A great manager can become one of the best friends you'll ever have.

There's a dark side to all of this. Hero worship is okay until you find out your idol has feet of clay. The rare manager who deserves to be a role model also deserves the benefit of realistic expectations.

Learning to accept your boss's flaws is an important part of achieving job satisfaction. Going around expecting him to be a deity means you will never have a positive relationship with him. Balance the flaws against his good points. If the scales tip in the right direction, leave it at that. Remind yourself that having another human being for a boss is the best you are going to do in this lifetime.

It will help to look at your boss in the context of the demands and pressures she faces on the job. Sometimes really intolerable behavior on the part of the boss is temporary. It results from some passing outside pressure and with a little patience on your part will go away.

Be careful of judging the boss harshly on the subject of fairness. A good boss must be fair, but understand that the boss must also be flexible. Fairness doesn't mean that everyone will be treated exactly the same way. What it means is that the boss will give everyone the same opportunities, and give each person the amount of direction and attention he or she needs to keep up productivity, motivation, and job satisfaction.

4

TALKING TO THE BOSS

I have this thing about authority, about walking right up to it and looking it squarely in the eye, about speaking right out to it bravely . . .

Joseph Heller
Something Happened

Let me tell you a story I heard at a management conference in New Jersey. A woman named Marian approached me during a break and said she wanted to explain to me how she was promoted from secretary to manager.

About a year earlier, she and her husband, a retired fireman from Piscataway, had realized their dream: after his retirement, they had bought a sporting goods store. They knew that at first the store wouldn't make enough money to support them. But with his retirement pay and her secretary's salary they figured they could get along until the business began to show a profit. She planned to keep her job in a local tobacco company for a while. As soon as the store brought in enough money, she planned to quit her job and work full-time with her husband. In about six months, they were at a really frustrating point for her. She loved working in the store on weekends and hated the nonsense she had to put up with in her corporate job. But they still needed at least part of her salary to pay their monthly bills.

A friend suggested the perfect answer: Marian needed to get herself fired. That way, they could use her unemployment check to supplement the store's income, and she would be free to put all her energies where she wanted them.

Although at first she thought the idea absurd, before long Marian saw it as her best bet. She set out to get laid off. She knew she had to do this carefully. She was afraid if she did something outrageous they would fire her for cause and she wouldn't get her unemployment check. She decided the best way to get laid off was to be just slightly obnoxious.

From then on, she started to tell her boss whenever he gave her a dumb assignment. She told him when she disagreed with him. She said things like, "You know, Harry, if you really wanted to do something smart, you'd send this project to an outside printer instead of having me spend half a day at the copying machine." She considered her behavior insubordinate. She thought her boss would call her lazy. She waited for the ax to fall.

Her scheme didn't work. Her boss liked her thinking. The more she spoke her mind, the more he sought her ideas. Eventually, he promoted her to office manager. Now she loves her job, and her husband is getting along in the store with hired help.

Even though she never intended it, talking to the boss improved Marian's situation at work. Think what you can do if you direct your efforts to that goal.

The problem for most people is getting the motivation or the courage to do it. You may feel safer keeping your complaints from the boss. Instead, you and your friends can hold a symposium on job problems next Friday at noon at the local Pizza Hut. That would be therapeutic, for the moment. But if you want to improve the situation, you probably have to discuss the issues with your boss. Here are some thoughts to help you get up the nerve.

WHY YOU NEED TO
TALK TO THE BOSS

First, only you can get across your own point of view. Your boss can't read your mind. Even if she tries, she may read you wrong. If you try holding things in, you will unintentionally broadcast that something is eating you. The sour look on your face, your skimpy job performance, or your bickering or snide remarks will betray you. Most bosses will interpret such behavior as *your* personality problem, *your* lack of job motivation stemming from *your* own personal difficulties, and definitely as *your* lack of potential. To avoid sending these unintentional messages, you need to send clear, intentional ones through planned conversation.

Holding in your complaints can be dangerous in other ways, too. It certainly will drain your energy. Keeping your mouth shut can be much more difficult than speaking up. And if you haven't got the nerve to say something, you can always tell yourself that you are keeping quiet to be polite. Baloney. If you're too scared to speak up, or if you're afraid that making waves will get you into trouble, that's all right with me. Just don't try to pass off your reluctance as good manners or wisdom.

Procrastinating about these discussions almost

inevitably makes them more difficult. A minor issue that would have been easy to discuss calmly can become a major source of disgust. If you put it off until you can't stand it, your emotions may get so exaggerated that you cannot come across as a rational person.

Overly emotional outbursts will get you a reputation as a hothead. No one, least of all management, will want to listen to your hysterical complaints. There is often only a thin line between courage and craziness. From a distance it may be hard to tell which side you're on. Don't go to war over trivialities, and don't let your emotions run away with you.

The psychologist Fritz Perles said that some people save up their little hurts like trading stamps. If you insult them by not saying good morning, they don't tell you about it; they put a stamp in their book. If you forget to send them a copy of a memo, they don't ask for it; but they remember it. And so on. And on. Until finally the little book is full of stamps. Then they cash in the whole thing at once. They explode in a tirade of accusations and descriptions of old wounds.

If you take this approach, you will end up overwrought. You will come across as a person so mired in trivia, so outraged by petty issues, that you can't concentrate on the larger problems of life or work. It may seem silly to "have a talk" because someone didn't invite you to a luncheon, but it is better, if it really bugs you, to bring it up as a minor issue and get it over with. Your other sane choice is to forget it (I mean really forget it).

If you save it up, you're probably in for a shouting match with the boss just before you quit (or get fired). Know yourself; if you aren't going to be able to forget it, talk about it right away.

Besides, letting the situation become overly emotional and tense will do nothing for your health—mental or physical. Losing your composure will increase your level of stress and decrease your credibility.

Don't give your boss any ammunition to use against you. The boss can use your "unreasonable" behavior as an excuse for his shenanigans. If you are so outraged by what has happened to you, give yourself a chance to cool off before you talk about it. During the cooling-off period, set your objectives, decide what you want to accomplish and why, and plan your strategy. This will help you keep your anger from getting in your way.

PREPARE YOURSELF
TO SUCCEED

Think out your approach to the boss. First, be very clear about what you want. "Improvement" is not a clear objective. Neither is a raise. Suppose you insist on having another assistant and the boss sends you his nephew, J. Pierpont Slothful, who turns out to be more trouble than he's worth. Or you ask for a raise and he says "yes" and then gives you $1.50 a week. Either way, the boss will say you got your way; you won't agree. Before you talk to the boss, think out exactly what you want, what qualities it must have, and how much of it you need. Give some specific dimension to your request.

Be selective about what you ask for. If you go to the boss with a list of fifty-three things that absolutely must happen in the next twenty-seven hours you are going to give the boss a headache and an excuse to dismiss all of your requests as absurd. Decide on your priorities and start with the most important thing on the list. The boss probably has limited time to spend on your needs, limited patience for dealing with your troubles, and a limited capacity to change his or her own behavior.

For particularly reluctant or difficult bosses, you may want to start by talking about something the boss will easily accept. For instance, if your boss is a stickler for the budget and your highest priority item is something that requires a budget variance, forego that issue for the moment. Focus on something that the boss can do without spending any money. Later, as your relationship with your boss improves, you can bring up the touchier questions. When you get a good response, express your gratitude and enthusiasm. If you want a warm welcome the next time you go to the boss with a request, you'd better make sure you say thank you this time.

Once the first change takes hold or the first promise is delivered, give the boss a little breathing space before you hit him with your next appeal. Old habits die hard; you don't want to seem relentless in your requests or insensitive in your timing. You may be desperate to relieve some of your own stress, but your success may depend on waiting a spell before you begin your next campaign.

Before you approach the boss, test your idea. Are your expectations realistic? Even if your request is valid in your eyes, will the boss be able to see the logic in it? Where will the boss's resistance come from? What in the boss's perspective will make it difficult for him to accept your proposal? How can you make the idea more palatable? Can you present your idea in a more positive light? Care at this juncture can pay great dividends.

Psych out the boss before you make your approach. Think about the boss's needs, objectives, strengths, and weaknesses. Your boss's goals may affect the reception you get. Without prying, find out what those goals are. If you can't discuss them openly with the boss, you may speculate on what they are. But remember, your assumptions are assumptions. Don't take them for fact; your boss isn't a mind reader and neither are you.

Think of the pressures your boss may be feeling from *his* boss. Ted Mill, for instance, wanted his boss to make an exception to a rule. Ted supervised the accounting staff at the corporate headquarters of a Chicago supermarket chain. The company rule said that a person had to be in his job for more than six months to qualify for a vacation. One of Ted's new clerks, Betsy Granger, who had been on the job only four months, had a pass to fly for free to California, but the pass would expire before she was eligible to take time off. She asked Ted to make an exception to the policy and allow her to take a week off.

Ted was pleased with Betsy's work and wanted to encourage her. When he went to his boss, he was confident he'd get the okay to let her go. Bob Penton, the department manager, was a flexible guy and usually went along with Ted's judgment on such questions. This time, he shocked Ted by not only turning him down but by lecturing him for ten minutes on what he called Ted's slack management style. Ted wondered if Bob was losing his grip. What Ted didn't know was that Bob had just received a ranking out from his own boss, who had accused Bob of not maintaining tight enough control. Ted never found out why his simple request received such a nasty response.

If they aren't temporarily out of sorts for some reason, most bosses respond very well to appeals that consider the best interests of the whole company. Think beyond the confines of what will benefit you personally or your department or group. If it's good for you and bad for the company, you know what the boss will say. Find a way to present your request in its best light. Let's use Ted's request as an example. Assume for the moment that the deck is not stacked against Ted, that Bob's feelings on bending policy are neutral at the moment. Ted has two possible ways to plead his case with Bob. He could do it on the basis of being nice to Betsy—he could say, "Betsy's a sweet kid and she doesn't have that much money. I don't know when she'll ever get another chance to go to California. I think we should be nice guys and let her go." That might work. But consider this alternative—Ted says, "Betsy is very motivated and productive. I think we can maintain her high level of commitment and enhance her value to the company if we show her that we can be considerate of her as a person. The rest of the staff know this is a special case. I'm sure it would put us in a good light with them as well if we make an exception in Betsy's case." The latter appeal clearly makes it easier for Bob to feel businesslike about saying yes.

If you are unsure of what your boss's attitudes are, ask. Your theories about the inner workings of the boss's mind may be fascinating, but they probably have little to do with reality. The further off base they are, the more likely you are to get tagged out. Check out your assumptions.

Be prepared to put your ideas in perspective, to introduce your suggestion with a little background. People often overestimate what the boss already knows. Especially if your boss used to do your job, you may imagine that she remembers it in all of its detail. But things may have changed since the boss did your job. Don't drown her in a long recounting of the obvious, but don't assume too much.

Look for a common ground. If you are disgusted with your boss because he's a slob or she's a perfectionist, you may be so distracted by your differences that you ignore the goals you have in common. Remember that you are looking for an *agreement*. You need to start with what you agree on already and negotiate on the basis of mutual gain.

Looking for agreements will allow you to present yourself and your ideas in the most attractive way. Keep your attitude positive. If you assume that everything the boss does and says will be poison, you will poison your own chances by making a negative presentation. Begin by thinking that both you and the boss can win. If you cannot be optimistic, it may be too late to improve your situation. In that case, talking things over with the boss may be just a formality. It will definitely be an exercise in frustration. Hopeless is hopeless. But if you have hope that things can improve, keep that optimistic picture in mind.

One more time: You are trying to change the boss's behavior, not the boss's personality. You are looking for small changes over time. It might be nice if the boss suddenly realized what a dunce she's been and transformed herself from Lady Macbeth into Joan of Arc. Historically, a few people have been suddenly transformed after hearing angels' voices. But only a few. And you are not an angel.

Consider also the form of your communication. Notice how the boss communicates. This will tell you what style of communication appeals to him. If your boss uses free-form discussions to reach mutually acceptable decisions, he may feel pressured if you go in with a conclusion, recommendation, and rationale all laid out.

Watch the way your boss reacts to other people's communications as well as your own. If one of your colleagues goes into great detail at a meeting and your boss doodles on her pad or looks at his fingernails, you can conclude that brevity will be more appealing. One engineer in a utility company needed two chances to learn what the chief engineer preferred. He went to the boss and stated a problem, describing the debacle in all of its putrid details. Then he sat there waiting for the chief engineer to tell him what he should do to solve the problem. Instead the boss asked a question, "What do you want me to do?"

A couple of months later, after describing another issue to his boss, the engineer heard the same question, "What do you want me to do?" The next time and every time after that, the engineer gave a brief description of the problem and recommended an action plan for solving it. His relationship with his boss improved immensely.

Make your message appealing. Some people's brains seem to be wired to respond to visual information. If you show them a picture of the old cars in the company fleet, they'll listen more openly to mileage data and maintenance costs. Other people seem programmed for audio input. They don't want to read about the poor service you've been getting from a supplier; they'd rather hear your war stories. Some psychologists say you can tell which people are which by the way they talk. Visual people will say, "I see what you mean." Audio people will say, "I hear what you're saying." Every boss has quirks and preferences. What worked like magic with your last boss may derail you with the one you have now.

When a new president took over a division of a packaged-goods company, clashes in style abounded. The old president had been a listener.

To present ideas to him, people wrote sparse outlines of their proposals and sat around the conference room table with him, going over each point and answering his questions. The new president was a reader. When he took over, the old techniques drove him nuts. He hated making decisions on the spot. Having a report to read ahead of time gave him a chance to think over the question before someone demanded a yes or no answer. His people were puzzled and dismayed that he didn't buy their proposals. They were accustomed to a free exchange and this boss barely responded to their presentations. In the end, the boss himself realized what was needed. "Give me a couple of pages to read," he said. "I promise if I get a report at least four hours beforehand I will have read it by the meeting. Getting it the night before would be even better. If I've read the information ahead of time, I can ask intelligent questions and be prepared to make a decision."

Your boss may not be as explicit as the one in this story. You may need to ask or figure out the best approach.

Whatever style of communication you use, don't lose the boss's attention. Studies put the attention spans of middle managers at three to nine minutes. That means you have less than ten minutes to get your points across before your boss becomes distracted—by the phone, another meeting, random thoughts evoked by something you said. All of a sudden the boss's mind is on something else and you've lost it. Plan your attack so that the major part of what you have to communicate—in writing or in person—can be absorbed in less then ten minutes.

Watch your timing. Choose a moment when the boss has the time and the mental and psychological energy to listen. If he is about to attend an important conference or is waiting for the birth of his first child, you may find him too distracted. Then there are the bosses who find it convenient never to have time to spend with their subordinates. Timing with this type of boss will be tricky if not impossible. Do your best. With Herb Baldwin, for instance, Ann Mannello's patience was sorely tried. Whenever she asked to talk to him, he'd say, "Yeah, yeah. Good idea, but . . ." And he'd mention some urgent business as an excuse for not seeing her. Herb and Ann worked in the marketing department at a copying machine company. Ann was an assistant product manager who was trying to get Herb to clarify her objectives. She felt her questions were vital; Herb said he agreed, but he was always distracted.

When she first asked, he set up a time with her, but got a last-minute, urgent call from the division president. He canceled his meeting with Ann. Then he put her off because he was getting ready for the annual sales meeting. Then he needed to prepare a critical presentation to top management. Then he had to clean things up before he went on vacation. Then he had to catch up on the work that had piled up while he'd been away.

In the meantime, Ann became more and more insecure. She was working hard on a number of projects, but she wasn't sure she was doing the right things. The closer it got to her annual performance appraisal, the more nervous she became. She was afraid Herb would play the old game of "shoot first, we'll hold up the target later."

At last, she saw how she could trap Herb. They had a trip planned to New York to visit their ad agency. Ann made sure they were booked on the same flight in adjoining seats. She even sat in the smoking section for this occasion.

As soon as the no smoking light went out, Ann pulled out a draft of her objectives. "Herb," she said, "now that we have some time together when we can't be interrupted, let's go over my objectives. I need your okay on this list I've drawn up so I can be sure I'm putting my energy into the things you think are most important." Herb had the window seat; Ann was on the aisle. There was nowhere he could go.

Watch the geography, too. You will need privacy. If your boss is a bully, try to meet on neutral ground—not your office or hers, but a conference room or a restaurant—somewhere where no one has the upper hand, where you can feel more like equals. This may help the boss see you as a human being. It will also help you feel like one. Try anything that will give you confidence, including wearing your best business clothes.

Plan the meeting. One young woman felt she did her best speaking extemporaneously. She decided her big talk with the boss should be spontaneous. It was—his spontaneous thoughts on everything and no time for the important issues she wanted to discuss. If your boss has a nomadic mind, type up a brief agenda. Words written on pieces of paper tend to take on a life of their own. They can be the stabilizing influence, just the road map you need to get you to your destination.

When you invite the boss to the meeting, make it sound like an important business discussion. Say something like, "I'd like to discuss how things are going on the job and how I think we can improve our productivity." If you say you want to discuss problems with the way things are going, the boss will feel like she's being invited to the Spanish Inquisition. No one, not even a card-carrying jerk, would show up for that voluntarily.

Have the facts with you. Don't plan on presenting them all, but bring along the information you need to prove your points.

Practice. What? Practice? Yes, practice. Go over the meeting in your mind. Have a rehearsal with someone who can play the boss for you. It might be interesting to have the friend pretend he or she is the boss in a bad mood and in a good mood. One caution on this technique: it is a double-edged sword. It will allow you to go over your spiel and your answers to the boss's questions and to see yourself doing it in a nonthreatening atmosphere. This will set you up to succeed by making the practice session fun. All to the good. On the other hand, be careful not to expect that the boss will actually act the way your friend does. Too definite an expectation, especially a negative one, can color your approach and force you into the self-fulfilling prophecy.

The self-fulfilling prophecy is an important

concept. Basically it means that if you expect a positive outcome from some activity, you will unconsciously do a lot of little things that will help you succeed. Conversely, if you expect a negative outcome, the small, subconscious, negative things you do will spoil everything. Let me give you an example. I learned about this concept by watching what happened to a fellow participant at a week-long human interaction course in Maine.

Sixteen of us, strangers to one another, had come from all over the United States and Canada to learn more about the way people communicate. Registration was on Sunday afternoon. Several of us met while walking to the building where we would live and work for the next week. It consisted of a large, central lounge-conference room with two wings of bedrooms—one side for men and the other for women. Meals would be served down the hill at the dining room.

One of the participants—a tall, warm, and jolly bear of a man, a city planner from Montreal—extended an invitation. "I've got a jug of wine. Why don't we meet in the lounge forty-five minutes before dinner, have a drink, and walk down the hill together. Pass the word along to any of the others you run into."

At the appointed time, about eight of us gathered and introduced ourselves to one another. We were sitting at one end of the long, narrow room chatting when the door opened. A woman, who we later learned was named Barbara, stuck her head in the door, looked at us, wrinkled up her nose, and left.

"I wonder what's bothering her," someone said.

"Well, I guess we have at least one stuck-up person in the group," someone else remarked. We all agreed that we weren't going to let her spoil the conference for us.

Later at dinner, we sat together. Barbara sat apart, reading an important-looking green leather-bound book and obviously making sure she paid very little attention to us. Our response was to notice her, make a few remarks about her odd behavior, and then to ignore her.

The conference began in earnest on Monday morning. Barbara participated in the exercises, but made no effort to fit in with what very quickly became a close-knit group. We all assumed she preferred to go it alone, and we let her. Until Wednesday. In the middle of an exercise involving group dynamics Barbara started to cry. "People just don't like me," she said. "None of you likes me. I know that. I knew you wouldn't. When I first got here Sunday night, I saw you all sitting together and I wanted to join in, but I was sure you wouldn't like me so I didn't bother to try. Later that evening in the dining room, you all sat together and nobody invited me to sit with the group."

I was stunned. That wrinkled nose we had seen on Sunday evening was an expression of pain, an anticipation of rejection, not the look of disdain we had all thought it was. Barbara's big green book was a defense against loneliness. Barbara did many things to defend herself against the rebuff she was sure would come. And everyone of them helped to insure her rejection. What she foresaw was what she got.

In the end, we all understood Barbara and loved her for her courage in confronting her problem. Thanks to her, we all learned a precious lesson.

When you approach your boss plan well enough so that you can be confident and optimistic. If you anticipate a negative reaction, think through how you will deal with it so you can keep a positive outlook about the final outcome.

HOW THE BOSS MAY REACT

Typically people go through three steps in responding to a problem.

First, they say there is no problem.

Second, they admit there is a problem, but they refuse to accept any responsibility for it.

Third, they admit there is a problem and that there is something they can do about it.

Notice that at no point in this process can we be sure they'll admit that the problem is their fault. Some people may do this, but you can't count on it, especially from someone who thinks being in charge means always being right.

Expect your boss to go through these steps. At each step your objective should be to get him to the next step. Don't look for self-incrimination or remorse. That only happens in the movies. Set up the situation so that a calm, businesslike discussion will satisfy both of you and allow each of you to complete the task with dignity.

Be prepared to deal with shock. Your boss may be sincerely surprised by the difficulties you recount. Remember the dangers in reading the boss's mind and taking your assumptions for gospel. She may be stunned by what you have to say.

Kathy Solarey is the mother of four, including a two-year-old. Her boss assumed Kathy would not want to travel on business. Therefore, when he was picking people to work at the company booth at a convention in New Orleans, he did not ask Kathy to go. Instead he asked two other people, both single, who had joined the department after Kathy did. Kathy was angry to find that two people with less seniority were getting what she considered a perk. She would have loved to have had a few days away from the kids, especially at company expense. She felt passed over. When Kathy told her boss how she felt, he was genuinely surprised. Kathy, however, assumed the shock was feigned, or worse, a sign of complete insensitivity on the boss's part.

Your boss's reaction to what you have to say may also come from embarrassment or nervousness. If emotionally charged situations make you a little flustered, they undoubtedly do the same to your boss. Hard as it is to believe, your boss really is a human being. If he is nervous and overreacts, don't let it steam you up. Your hopes for a peaceful solution could evaporate in the resulting heat. Be brave and patient and keep working at it.

TECHNIQUES FOR GOOD COMMUNICATION

Use all the skill you have to get the best possible response from the boss. It's probably not a bad idea to review some general techniques of effective communication here. You know most of these and undoubtedly practice many of them by habit, but hearing about them again will give you confidence that you do know how to communicate well. Some of them will be reminders of things you don't always remember to do. Others will be new ideas that will get you over rough spots you haven't handled so well in the past.

First of all, pick fair topics for discussion. You can bring up the boss's communication with you or your need for information and feedback on your work; you can talk about work flow, the organization, your future, how someone else's behavior affects your work. Never bring up personalities— yours, the boss's, or anyone else's. You are not conducting a therapy session. Even if you are a Ph.D. psychologist, fully qualified to psychoanalyze your boss, don't do it. If you lack a degree in psychology, you have no business analyzing anyone. Your objective in these meetings is to prevent your boss from being a menace to you, not to become a menace yourself. Keep yourself honest by talking about people—yourself, the boss, your coworkers, your subordinates—in terms of what they do and what they don't do, not in terms of what they are or are not. Talk about behavior, not character. Let me say that again, talk about behavior, not character.

Don't come across as judge. To be diplomatic, just follow these two simple rules. When you have something positive to say (and you'd better find something) be very specific. Don't say, "You communicate with me very well." Say: "You always give me all the information I need to understand the customer's needs. With the National Trust order, for instance . . ." If you have a complaint, talk about it in the future tense. Rather than recount the boss's misdeeds of the past, which cannot be changed, talk about what you would like to see happen in the future. Don't say, "You never invite me to the Friday management meetings." Say: "I'd like to come to the Friday management meetings. I think I can make a contribution when the group discusses . . ."

Avoid emotional outbursts. There are certain topics or even words that you know will set your boss off. Work around them, or if you must raise them, work up to them.

Be honest. Be real. Authenticity will pay off for you. Your boss will sense it if you try to put on a personality or characteristic that is not your own. She'll disbelieve you or question your sincerity.

Beware of misunderstandings. In many problem-solving discussions, emotions run high. Misinterpretations and miscommunications are bound to happen. If your boss says something that puzzles you (and especially if it outrages you), explain to him what you thought you heard. If your boss seems to react very emotionally when you think you've said something quite neutral, make sure the boss understands you. Not all disagreements result from misunderstandings, but the ones that do are a total waste of energy. Check to make sure communication is accurate. It's worth the trouble.

Listen.

Watch your body language. And watch your boss's. Jackie Crew had a boss who always tried to show a poker face. He had spent years as a personnel interviewer and developed quite a knack for hiding his feelings, he thought. Jackie didn't notice it at first, but his body language gave him away. When Jackie went to see him with a new idea one day, he started to play with his tie. She didn't read the cue but went on. Then her boss swiveled around in his chair and looked at Jackie over his left shoulder. Jackie persisted. At last, he looked out the window and started playing with his tie again. When she was finished with what she had to say, the boss told Jackie he would consider her suggestion and get back to her. She never heard about it again.

Eventually Jackie learned to interpret the boss's body language. When his hand reached for his tie, she changed her line of attack. When he swiveled around in his chair, she asked him how he felt about what she was suggesting. When he looked out the window and reached for his tie, she beat a swift but graceful path to the nearest door.

Some communications experts say you can

build rapport by matching your communication style and body language to that of the person you are speaking to. They say you should match their voice level and tempo, breathing rate, body posture and movements. I have noticed that when I'm really in mental sync with someone, these things seem to match automatically. I guess doing this consciously can help the flow of communication. What I don't advise is matching negative nonverbal signals. For instance, if the boss shouts or folds her arms, don't you do it, too.

Be specific. When you approach the boss with a problem, direct your remarks to one situation. Say precisely what is wrong and what you want to do about it. Give a couple of examples if you like, but don't go back to ancient history and don't overkill with anecdotes about what a tough time you're having.

Approach the meeting with as positive an outlook as you can muster. Beforehand, picture it in your mind; create a mental image of you and the boss calmly discussing the issues; see yourself sitting in the conference room or office feeling confident and positive. Keep a picture in your mind of the meeting ending with smiles on both your faces. The more afraid you are of the outcome, the more important it is for you to imagine the boss will be in the best of all possible moods that day. Imagine that he will have just heard some very good news about his own future. This may seem a trivial piece of advice; I consider it the most important in this chapter. Remember what we said about the self-fulfilling prophecy. If your frame of mind is negative, you're unlikely to accomplish anything positive for yourself or anybody else.

Meet the boss as an equal. If you whine like a victim, you'll invite victimization; if you present yourself as an impotent sufferer, you'll be dubbed an unworthy wimp. A straightforward approach laced with a little humor and a lot of tact will make the most successful presentation of your point of view.

But tell the truth. Larry Shimkin knew his boss, Georgia Fidelio, was a stickler for control. It was her favorite word. When Georgia decided to delay implementing a new capital expenditure approval system, she asked Larry to poll the department heads to find out how they felt about the delay. Larry already knew they would hit the ceiling. They had already started to prepare their reports to conform to the new system. But Georgia insisted that he ask.

The response was what he expected—mutiny was imminent. When he described the potential problems to her, he could see Georgia starting to boil. He didn't want her to get mad at him. "I guess," he said, "it could get pretty bad, but I'm sure it's nothing we couldn't control." When Larry said the magic word, Georgia calmed down. They both felt a lot better, until three weeks later, that is, when the postponement was announced. Nearly every department head in the company blamed Larry for Georgia's bad decision. Perhaps they were right. Larry's willpower failed him when it came to delivering the truth. He never told Georgia about his worst fears. When they came true, Georgia blamed him for the lack of control that ensued.

Try to strike a balance between too much doom and gloom and a whitewash. If you apply too much pressure, the boss will reject what you are saying. People can become very suspicious of the hard sell. If you try to rush the boss into a decision without allowing time for due consideration, she may balk and you may lose your opportunity entirely.

Don't make the discussion too one-sided. Acknowledge the boss's point of view. For instance, if you have to interrupt the boss when he's having trouble with budget approvals, say, "I know this is coming at a tough time in the middle of budgeting, but I think it's important enough that you would want to discuss it." The boss will listen better and be more empathetic if you demonstrate that you are an understanding person yourself. You can be single-minded in your determination to solve the problem without being narrow-minded in your viewpoint.

Show that you understand both sides, but then demonstrate how the scales tip in favor of your preferred course of action. This should extend to any criticism you have of how the boss is managing you. Be particularly careful to thank the boss for those things that have been helpful. If you have to ask for more direction, don't say, "You never tell me what my goals should be." It's better to begin with, "I like the fact that you give me independence to make my own decisions; it helps me learn and take on more responsibility." Then you can go on to say, "There are times, however, when I feel I need more guidance."

When the boss responds to what you say, listen not only to the spoken message but also to the hidden message.

Be prepared to trade off. You need to have a clear idea of what you want, but stay flexible. Your boss has a viewpoint. Some of the best solutions will be neither hers nor yours but ones that satisfy both your needs. You won't be able to discover what those mutually agreeable ideas are if you are rigid about your requests.

Come out of the meeting with an action plan. If the boss accepts what you say and gives you an open-minded hearing, you may be on your way to a solution to the problem. Get the boss to agree that you will write up a summary of what each of you must do.

Make a date to get together again. Time your next meeting to conform with some milestone in accomplishing your mutual plan of action. Put a date on the calendar right away. Once you have opened up the channels of communication, you will want to keep them open and make these meetings seem like business as usual (as they should be). Otherwise, if you run into further problems, you will have to open the whole subject again. You want these discussions to be part of an ongoing process. If you wait until something breaks down, you will seem like a complainer who keeps calling a meeting any time a trivial problem occurs.

DEALING WITH
THE BOSS'S RESISTANCE

You may find that your boss resists the ideas you are suggesting or denies that there is a problem at all. This sort of response is normal at first. As we said earlier in this chapter, people sometimes begin by denying the problem. Your boss may resist the issue in other ways. A straightforward "no" may seem cruel, but at least it is clear and clean. You can deal with it. Ask the boss why she objects. This will either give you ammunition for counter arguments or tell you how deep-seated the boss's resistance is.

Some bosses will resort to shoddy stratagems to block you. Tom Hawthorne wanted to say no when his secretary asked him to upgrade her job. She said he had increased her responsibilities without increasing her status or her pay. He didn't believe her. But he was afraid that if he said so she would work less diligently or resent him or cry. So he told her he would do what he could. He wrote a memo to the personnel department vaguely mentioning that many secretaries were undervalued in the current salary administration system. He asked for nothing special for his assistant. He never followed up.

This sort of passive resistance is common. The boss complies with the demand, but just barely and with no real intention of redressing the grievance.

Jay Benton's boss pulled a similar side-step.

He just put things off. He listened intently to Jay's request that they define more clearly who had what responsibilities. He was sympathetic. "I know this is bothering you a great deal, Jay, and I want to deal with it as soon as I can. I promise you we'll get on it as soon as we finish with strategic planning." But after strategic planning, there was a reorganization of the field force and after that office redecoration and on and on.

The stall, when it is used by a boss determined to avoid an issue, is one of the best weapons in today's changing work environment. Some postponements are legitimate. But some are just excuses, and anyone looking for an excuse can easily invent one.

Pat Knotter had an interesting variation on the stall. Whenever one of the credit analysts in her department at the bank made a suggestion for change, she expressed great enthusiasm. "Wow," she'd say, "that's just the kind of creative thinking we need around here. I'm so happy you came to me with this idea." The problem was that she never took any action on any of the recommendations. Sometimes she followed up with the favorite side-step of cowardly managers everywhere: "It's a great idea, but top management would never approve."

Karen Chesire worked for a plumbing supply company where the owner couldn't blame top management. He *was* top management. Instead he used the "it's my turn" tactic. His basic response was to ask his employees to "give in on this one."

He always promised to remember their loyalty. But his memory was faulty. He remembered some things and not others. For instance, when Karen took a legitimate day off to accompany her son on a school trip, he remembered it and acted as if he had given her a gift instead of a vacation day she had coming to her. When she complained about her postponed raise, he told her she owed him one for his "flexibility." Somehow the accounts never balanced. Karen always owed the boss.

"That's not the way we do it here." "This is an imposition on me." "You are being unfair." "You are not a team player." There are many ways the boss can put you off. The best way to deal with these tactics is to try to get at the underlying reasons for the boss's resistance and to deal with them. Another way is to call polite attention to the tactic. It's best to say, "you keep putting off the reorganization you promised. I sense that you really don't want to do it." This may or may not get you what you want. At the very least it will put the boss on notice that you know what's going on.

I strongly advise that you use the most straightforward methods you can in dealing with your boss, however slippery he is. Be prepared to recognize and have the courage to state your feelings and observations. Say what you see and how you feel about it. State what you think might be the boss's point of view and ask directly for what you want. You can then say sincerely, "I'm being straight with you and I want you to be straight with me." If you and your boss are willing to struggle, you may win out over the prevailing custom of politics and tacky tactics that pervades so many business relationships these days.

If you think I'm being harsh in judging modern business, take a look at what managers are reading. Books on management advise all manner of Machiavellian methods, from winning through intimidation to management by seduction. One advises managers to appeal to employee's insecurities. The author says a manager faced with a man who refuses to take on an assignment should appeal to the employee's masculine insecurities. The manager should say the employee doesn't have the guts to take on the challenge. Such sneak attacks could work on you if you allow yourself to react emotionally to psychological arm twisting. You could accept imprudent assignments. If the task is impossible, just remember it will be you, not your boss, who will wind up transferred to the sales office in Barrow, Alaska. Recognizing and dealing with these sly stratagems will be an invaluable skill, not only with bosses but with all manner of manipulators—brothers-in-law, eleven-year-old offspring, self-styled religious prophets, and next-door neighbors with broken lawnmowers.

THE SPECIAL CASE OF PERFORMANCE APPRAISAL

Getting the boss's attention and putting your points across may be difficult to arrange. In most large organizations, however, there is a built-in mechanism to make sure this happens at least once a year: the performance appraisal meeting. Every manager is supposed to meet with each employee at least once a year to review the employee's work performance. In some companies, there are elaborate (and often ridiculous) forms to fill out. The personnel department monitors the process. Usually the meeting, to its detriment, is inextricably intertwined with salary actions. Most employees view it as a time to be passive, to listen to the boss's appraisal, and to find out "how much they got."

Get smart about performance appraisal. Prepare yourself for the meeting. Go in ready, not for a fight, but to take an active part. Use the occasion to express your own opinions. What happens in that meeting can profoundly affect your future at work.

Keep a folder in your desk and throughout the year drop in it notes about special things you do, extenuating circumstances for mess-ups, anything you will want to remember when you prepare yourself for your appraisal meeting.

Prepare for the meeting by doing a self appraisal. Get a copy of the form your boss will use so you know the categories on which you will be judged. Don't take a defensive posture by trying to anticipate and counter the boss's criticisms. Rather, be prepared to give your own balanced appraisal of the work. Remember most of all that you are evaluating your work, not yourself as a person.

At the meeting, ask the boss's permission to talk first. Tell her that you have done a self-appraisal and that it might be a good jumping off point for your discussion. This will take a delicate touch because you won't want to look as if you're taking over the meeting. If your boss is very defensive she may object to an assertive stance. Without alienating her, do your best to get your major points out before she starts her evaluation.

Give a quick, balanced assessment. If you say only good things and say them all, you'll sound like a braggart. Besides, you will leave the boss nothing to say but criticisms. Take no more than five minutes. Don't expect the boss to sit still and listen to a half-hour soliloquy.

Use a direct, matter-of-fact tone. Remember, you are talking about the work. It is important to you. Show that you take it seriously. Don't talk about your character or personality; talk about what you did or didn't do. Admit your failures, and say how you plan to prevent them in the future.

When your boss is appraising your work, listen carefully. If the boss criticizes you and begins to turn the meeting into a discussion of your personality or character, keep calm. Direct the conversation to the work by asking for examples of things you did and didn't do. If your boss says you are unreliable and poor in judgment, it's going to be difficult for you to keep your seat. But the best response is to ask, "Can you give me a few examples of things I did or didn't do that drew you to these conclusions about me." Look right at the boss and wait for an answer. If your boss talks about nothing but your personality traits it may be that she has a mistaken idea of what a performance appraisal is supposed to be. Some bosses get a bum steer from the forms they have to fill out—forms which ask them to judge their employees on traits such as "cooperativeness." If this is the case in your company, try asking your boss to concentrate on what you've done, on evaluating the work, not your personality. The boss will probably feel more comfortable with that approach, too. Just say, "I feel uncomfortable if we sit here and talk about what kind of person I am. Can we make this a real *performance* evaluation? Let's talk about how well I do my work."

Concur with your boss's valid critiques. You can disarm the boss if you say, "Your criticism is correct. I was unhappy with the outcome of that project, too. Let's talk about how I can avoid such failures in the future." This will show the boss that you are confident in yourself and that you want to improve. If, instead, you are defensive and give excuses, you may hear that worst of all castigations—"You can't take criticism."

Ask for examples, especially if your boss says nothing positive. Ask what she liked about your performance. Some bosses think performance appraisal meetings are places to air their grievances. You may need to gently enlighten your boss on this subject. The vice, of course, is versa. If your boss gives only praise, ask if there is any way you can improve.

Handle your own emotions. You may find it hard to remain calm if the boss's criticism seems harsh. Try to think of his barbs as an attack on your actions, not an attack on you. Remember, if you can't hear another person's critique you cannot improve. In the end, you will decide whether or not you want to change your behavior. But if you don't listen to the feedback on your performance, you won't be able to make that choice.

Bring up the subject of your own career. The end of the appraisal meeting is a good time to talk about your ambitions, your needs, your motivations. You may not find it so easy to get the boss's time for such a discussion if you put it off for another meeting.

If there is an appraisal form in your company, your boss will fill it out and sign it and it will go into your personnel folder. It will probably be in there as long as you work for the company. You have a right to see that form. In fact, some companies require that you sign the form. If the form gives you a space for comments, make some. Even if you agree totally with what your boss has written, put in some words of your own. Show people who will read the form in the future that you are involved and interested and articulate enough to have something to say for yourself.

If you disagree with the boss's appraisal, evaluate the damage the boss's remarks can do. If you disagree on some trifle, let it pass. Work is no place for trivial pursuits. If you have a serious objection to the boss's evaluation, tell the boss how you feel and see if you can get the boss to change it. If your boss is filing an appraisal you consider unfair, follow the company's normal grievance procedure to redress the problem. That may mean that you will speak to your boss's boss or to someone in the personnel department. In this process, don't expect anyone to tell you that you are right and your boss is wrong. Even if the people you speak with believe your boss is in the ninety-ninth percentile of corporate wackos, they are unlikely to say that to you. What you want is an impartial hearing of your side of the story. Get some advice from your boss's boss or personnel on how you should handle the issue. If the advice is sensible, follow it.

Also write your own appraisal for your file. Don't make it an appraisal of your boss or a complaint about the ill treatment you have received. Just write what you want people to know about you and what you have accomplished for the company. Make sure that what you have written gets into the file to counterbalance what the boss has written.

SOME GENERAL THOUGHTS ABOUT COMMUNICATING WITH THE BOSS

Thus far, this chapter has been about problem solving. Given the nature of this book, that seems appropriate. But before we leave the subject of communication, here are a couple of pieces of advice about how to avoid problems.

Build your boss's confidence in you. Do I need to tell you to do your job and do it well? If your boss sees you as competent and hardworking, she will welcome your suggestions and be open to your requests. Trust is the only good foundation for a boss-subordinate relationship. If your boss is capable of trusting, do all you can to bolster her faith in you.

Make sure your boss notices what you are doing. Each month, write a one-page report of your accomplishments. Give the status of your work, and document your major accomplishments. (If you object and say you are not good at writing reports, I'll just tell you to learn how. Whose life are we talking about here anyway?) Keep copies of these reports to use as back-up or ammunition at performance appraisal time.

Make sure you understand what your boss expects. If he tends to be vague about assignments, find a way to get specific information. If you have to work under a lot of assumptions about what he wants, write your assumptions in a memo; send it to the boss and keep a copy. Then he can clear up any misconceptions you have before you go too far with them. Or you can use the memo as the basis for discussing the subject. Make sure the boss sees this as an attempt to do the job correctly, not just a safety net if you are later criticized for doing the wrong things. Of course, you can always fall back on the memo later if the boss says that you failed to meet his expectations.

Don't expect your boss to read your mind. If you need information, ask for it. This idea seems so simple you may wonder how I have the nerve to pass it off as an important piece of advice. But I have seen that, obvious as it is, it is often the last thing frustrated employees will think of doing. My friend Dick was beginning a three-day management training program for one of his clients—a major international consumer goods company. Many of the twenty or so participants seemed unenthusiastic about the session. Dick asked one—as it happened, a man who had traveled from Belgium to the United States for the program—if he was happy to be there. The answer was noncommittal. "Why did you come?" Dick asked. "Because I got a memo from my boss telling me to come," the man replied. That was it. He resented having to make the trip, and didn't know why his boss had nominated him for the training program. But he asked no questions. He had his orders and he marched—all the way to the airport to take a seven-hour flight to a destination on another continent. And he didn't know why he was going and he didn't want to go. But he went. Ridiculous.

Learn to question what the boss has said without questioning his authority. Even if you have a great boss, he can make mistakes or operate on misinformation. If what the boss says doesn't seem logical—if the boss tells you that your course in accounting is not covered by the company's tuition reimbursement plan or that the job in the marketing department is already filled—find a polite way to check it out. Your boss may be using old information or false assumptions. The issue may be critical to you, but of minor importance to the boss. He may not be motivated to check it out; you should be.

If, without overcompensating for the boss's

shortcomings, you can smooth communications, that's great. If you already have serious problems to solve, try to eliminate them through open communication. If all of your efforts fail, evaluate your position again. Make sure you have given the boss time to implement the changes you are requesting. It takes a while for people to turn themselves around. Look for signs of progress. If you see them and they encourage you, keep on track. If you lose hope that you and the boss will get it together, you will have to decide on your next step.

In some companies, it is easy to wait it out; things change rapidly. In one packaged goods company reorganizations are common. They seem to play music that only managers can hear. Every once in a while that music starts and several managers will get up and walk around for a while and all wind up in different chairs at the end of the day. This constant switching of managers from job to job means that people unhappy with their bosses needn't despair. If you don't like the one you've got, chances are that before the year is over you'll have a new one.

If your situation is intolerable and unlikely to change, give up and get yourself another job—either a transfer within the company or a new job entirely. If the fight is futile, accept defeat. Make your plans and get moving. If you have to stick around with the boss you have until you get a new job, remind yourself that you are a short-timer. That thought will keep you on an even keel until you can say good-bye. What a pleasure that will be.

This has been general advice on how to deal with bosses. The next several chapters will help you understand and deal with bosses in specific categories. Read on and see how many of the descriptions fit your boss.

5

IGNORAMUSES AND INCOMPETENTS

*Since when was a keen mind
anything but an obstacle to
promotion? It is mediocrity
and servility which are your
keys to the top.*

Beaumarchais
The Marriage of Figaro

*Adapted by
Richard Nelson*

At four o'clock on a sunny Friday afternoon in August, Mario Caso, a research chemist in a consumer products company, was finishing up a progress report and beginning to think about the beach. The weather report was good. He planned to take his wife and babies to the shore for the weekend. He hoped the traffic wouldn't be too bad that evening.

The phone rang. His department head, Phil Rhodes, had an emergency assignment. The company was about to launch a new advertising campaign that claimed their product had 40 percent less sugar than the competitors. The test commercial would air for the first time in Florida over the weekend. Three months earlier at a meeting, Phil had promised to have the claim verified in the lab. But he forgot to assign the test. Now, he was up against the legal department, which said the test had to be run before the commercial aired.

Phil didn't tell Mario any of this. All he told Mario was that he had to run the tests comparing the sugar content of the two products before he went home. After some low-key objections, Mario agreed, called home to tell his wife he would be late, soothed her disappointment about leaving that evening for the beach, and went to work on the test.

It was nearly seven o'clock before he finished.

He called Phil. He also tried the marketing department. And advertising. With the "emergency" assignment completed, he couldn't find anyone to listen to the report of his results. They had all gone home.

Forgetful bosses, ignorant bosses, and stupid bosses frustrate people and waste time and money. They cause ventures to fail, stockholders to loose their investments, and people to lose their jobs. Yet there are thousands of them. Heads of automobile companies admit that they don't know much about the internal combustion engine. Real estate millionaires are put in charge of departments of the government. The owner's son-in-law is given responsibility for advertising and public relations. Some people are assigned to jobs because the organization has a spare person and an open job. It becomes convenient to match them up regardless of the person's qualifications or aptitude. It takes care of the problem of what to do with old George.

Ignorant bosses hurt the company by making bad decisions. They hurt their employees by their incapacities. They can't teach their people anything or understand the difficulty of the assignments they make or guide their employees to success and satisfaction.

Some bosses are extremely well-versed in one area but ignorant in others. Penny Hall is a brilliant financial analyst. Her skill and knowledge in her field were renowned when she was put in charge of the research department of a brokerage firm. But she had concentrated on the technical aspects of her work to the exclusion of everything else. She knew nothing of personnel policies, office automation, or human psychology for that matter. Yet in her new job she had to make decisions about matters that profoundly influenced the working lives of the people in her department. When it came to choosing new computer equipment, she decided to ignore the advice of the head of administrative services because the equipment he recommended was made by a company whose economic future she questioned. She insisted that they purchase computers from another company, one she felt had a totally reliable financial future. The result was a totally unreliable computer system and eleven months of missed deadlines and flaring tempers.

When Penny dealt with the financial analysts that reported to her, she was fine. They didn't always approve of her desk-side manner, but they respected her competence and were dazzled by her skill and creativity. They all tried to think the way she did. But the rest of the department dreaded working with her. She didn't understand what was important to them, didn't even know what information they needed to do their work. What's more, she treated their requests for attention with annoyance. She seemed to feel they were a distraction from her "real" work.

Penny is smart; eventually she may learn. That's the nice thing about ignorance as opposed to stupidity. The difference is one of timing. Ignorance is temporary. Stupidity, unfortunately, is permanent.

Bill Heald is stupid. Nobody can figure out how such a feeble mind got a job as head of the education subsidiary of a publishing company. Some people say he was just the least obnoxious of the available candidates; others are convinced that he knows where the bodies are buried. Elaine Dennis doesn't care. She's just glad she got another job and away from Bill.

When she worked for Bill, Elaine was in charge of arranging management seminars. The company hired consultants to teach the seminars, rented hotel rooms, mailed out brochures, and registered people. Participants paid several hundred dollars apiece for the seminars, and the firm made its money on the difference between its costs and what was collected. Naturally, the better the attendance at the seminars the more money the company made.

When Elaine took over her job, the company was using about twelve consultants to teach the seminars. Most of them were people who had been around for a long time, people whose subject matters and approaches were outdated. A few were very new to the field and inexperienced. Both these groups charged less for their services than the top-notch consultants Elaine thought the job required. She put some new names on the roster. She chose people who could speak on popular topics and who had big names that would attract attention. They charged more, but their seminars drew large audiences and proved most profitable.

During an economic slump, registrations for all the programs dropped off and profits from the operation went down. Bill decided to cut costs. He told Elaine to cut out the more expensive consultants and keep the ones who charged the lowest fees. She argued that though they charged less, the cheaper consultants contributed very little to the bottom line. She recommended, instead, that they cut the unprofitable seminars, use new marketing strategies and spend some money on more appealing graphics for their brochures. Bill wouldn't listen. He insisted that the higher-priced consultants were overcharging. He wouldn't budge. Cost-cutting was his only tool. Eventually, Elaine yielded to his insistence. Registrations and profits from the operation dropped off to such a low that the company decided to phase out the seminars altogether. Elaine was on unemployment for three months before she found her new job.

Managers like Bill are a menace. Although they are unable to understand concepts instantly apparent to a six-year-old owner of a lemonade stand, being wrong doesn't slow them down. They don't know they're wrong; they don't know what they don't know. There is practically no problem so simple that it cannot confuse them.

They become mired in trivia, make mountains out of molehills, or, worse yet, molehills out of mountains. Detail drones can overdramatize insignificant issues, frustrate people, and waste their time with slavish attention to minor rules and procedures. They spend so much time paying attention to minutiae that they lose track of the obvious larger questions.

One report estimated that the average middle

manager wastes $12,000 worth of his or her own time each year. Imagine what the estimate would be if we extended that to include the employee time wasted by some of these low watt bulbs.

BEING NICE DOESN'T HELP

Bosses can be nice or nasty and brilliant or bumbling. The very best kind of boss to have is a nice and brilliant one. There are a few of those. Failing that, employees can often tolerate the stings of a nasty but brilliant boss because they can see his worth. Nasty nitwits are unbearable, and, fortunately, usually don't last very long—their personalities make it easy for people to squeeze them out one way or another. The hatred one feels for them is uncontaminated with guilt. It's the sweet ignoramuses that irk me most. Their behavior is so appealing that one feels reluctant to move against them or pressure them. Top management can be over-tolerant of these pleasant pea-brains.

It's common knowledge that people fear the unknown. The problem with ignorant bosses is that they know so little they fear nearly everything. Strangers, new procedures, and creative ideas are all grounds for them to divorce themselves from reality. Their suspicion is on a hair trigger.

Distrust makes it difficult for ignorant bosses to accept new information; and giving away information they already have sends them into fits. These bosses don't understand much about how the world operates, but they know that knowledge is power. They think the way to amass power is to hoard information. They don't use it as a medium of exchange, giving some to get some. Instead, they jealously guard every tidbit.

Merril Stanley worked for the controller of a film production company. Her boss, Jim, actually knew a great deal about what was going on in the company—no one would have called him ignorant. He was also very good at keeping the books. His boss, the president and owner of the firm, would have called him responsive. Whenever he asked Jim a question, he got an immediate answer. Jim told him everything he wanted to know, sometimes in too much detail.

But with everyone else in the company Jim was vague and evasive. Merril, as his secretary, was identified closely with him. She found it embarrassing when people made fun of him. Their favorite greeting was to ask her, "How are things at the Pentagon?" She felt it belittled her and her position, as well as Jim and his. She saw Jim's faults more clearly than anyone, but she didn't like to join in the criticism of her boss. She thought, *If I agree with everyone that my boss is a jerk, what does that make me?* She didn't know how to respond to the teasing. When the subject came up, she would usually find a reason to leave the room.

Her loyalty backfired. Her boss's tunnel vision kept her in ignorance and she was the one who suffered ultimately.

From time to time the firm negotiated loans to cover cash flow problems. Frequently, when they got contracts to do commercials or promotional films, they incurred expenses before they collected fees from their clients. This was normal in the industry and needing a loan didn't mean that the company was in trouble. But Jim, thinking himself wise and prudent, decided that the employees, including his own secretary, didn't need to know about such things. He never explained to Merril the purpose or importance of the loans. In fact, until one critical Thursday morning, Merril didn't know the loans existed.

That day, a series of events took place. Jim called in to say that his car had broken down and that he wouldn't be in until noon. He told Merril he was expecting an important call from the bank. When that call came in, she should give the bank manager some figures. He gave her the figures over the phone. He never told her what they represented and what their significance was. When she asked him about them, he acted as if she were prying into his private business. "Just give the numbers to the guy from the bank, Merril. You don't need to know more than that," he said.

Merril was hurt. She couldn't understand why Jim didn't trust her. She was loyal, and he knew it. Something told her she needed to know more. Yet he treated her questions as if they were idle curiosity or, worse yet, prying.

When the banker called at around eleven, Merril gave him the numbers. He questioned her closely about them, especially the ones Jim had said represented "contracts" and "debt." Merril didn't really understand what they meant but she knew it was important, so she tried to sound as knowledgeable as possible.

The following week, the firm needed the credit desperately to finish a project to meet a critical client deadline. At that point, the loan, which Jim and the president were sure was in the bag, was disapproved. The money wasn't available when the firm needed it, and the client deadline was missed. When the anger subsided and Jim investigated the issue, it turned out that the loan was disallowed because Merril had given the bank a wrong figure. Eventually the loan was approved, but only after a great deal of hubbub and embarrassment before the client. The president was livid . . . at Merril. He fired her on the spot. "Any idiot would have known that those figures were wrong," he told her. "If you've worked in a key position in this company for three and a half years and paid so little attention that you don't understand anything about our business, you don't deserve to work here." Jim never defended her. Later he told her there was nothing he could do.

Merril was upset and angry. She knew she wasn't stupid, but she felt stupid. And she knew she looked stupid to everyone around. *The other people in the firm know I'm being fired, she thought. They'll never really know why, but they'll figure out that I made a whopper of a mistake. And they'll be right. My big mistake was to be loyal to a boss who didn't trust me enough to give me information I needed to do my job.*

Merril's boss kept information to himself because he didn't trust anyone. Some bosses are just so lazy or distracted that they forget to tell their people things. Their heads are out there with

Captain Kirk. A personnel recruiter in a publishing company once complained to me that his boss never told him exactly what he wanted. "He expects that by some mysterious sorcery, I'll know. I'm not a magician. I probably couldn't read his mind, even if he had one."

Some bosses seem to expect that their people will have ESP. Others think they've already told people things when they really haven't. Still other bosses hesitate to make demands or give orders. Rather than making direct requests, they drop hints about what they want. If the boss is "too polite" to ask the people to do the work and the employees are too cautious to take the initiative themselves, nothing gets done.

In fact, incompetence in communication is the worst flaw in a boss. Only through open communication can employees understand what needs to be done so they can do it. This, of course, is basic and critical. It doesn't even get to the role of communication in generating enthusiasm for the work, maintaining employee motivation, and promoting employee development. A boss who can't communicate is a menace.

THE PRICE OF
MANAGERIAL INCOMPETENCE

Inability to communicate and other forms of managerial incompetence result in inefficiencies of all kinds. And inefficiency doesn't come cheap. In fact, it costs a great deal. Ignorant or incompetent managers make bad decisions. They cause the catastrophes that put their employees on the spot or on the unemployment line. In the extreme, employees can get sick or die.

If your boss is uninformed or incapable, at the very least you learn nothing. And this lack of growth can mean career stagnation. Ignorant bosses can stall your career even if you are top-notch at your job. They do this by being unable to evaluate your worth. In fact, in evaluating employees, a little bit of knowledge can be treacherous—for the employee, not the boss.

Watch out for the boss who is a one factor theorist. He's the one who has a firm grasp of one idea he uses in lieu of real knowledge, logic, and instinct. These bosses usually get into positions of power because they have a special skill or in-depth knowledge. You can trust their judgment in that area—you can learn from them about their special subject. But if the boss really is an idiot savant, be very careful when she gets into other areas. You may have to learn to guide her away from making false assumptions. Some bosses who are singular experts in one field know their limitations and are happy to delegate tasks of which they know nothing. Others, though, become enamored with being "the expert." They think they know everything about everything and meddle where they can do only damage.

Bosses are supposed to help us keep things moving, but some bosses are sources of delays and crises. Nancy Ermann was such a boss. Barry Mulqueen worked for her in the audio-visual production department of a giant insurance company. At any given moment they had projects going on with ten or twelve different departments. Juggling priorities was a major issue for their group. But Nancy allowed herself to be influenced by anyone who would take her to lunch. Heads of departments from around the company convinced her to give their project a higher priority. Whenever she suddenly called Barry into her office after a long phone conversation or a luncheon, he knew what was coming.

At first, he believed Nancy. He would listen to her description of the plight of the group health plans department, would accept her pronouncement that their work needed to be given a higher priority, and would shift the schedules of his staff. Often this meant taking people off one project and putting them on another. Sometimes he had to cancel one rush printing order and substitute another. He ran himself ragged trying to accommodate his boss and the "emergency" in the other department. But the priorities shifted with the wind.

Soon Barry found himself ordering a drink at lunch everyday and stopping for another on his way home. His consumption of cigarettes and coffee doubled in a two-month period. His staff began to complain to him about the chaotic scheduling. They told him they were disappointed in their own performance. The best they could do was rudimentary work, which they finished in the nick of time. He sympathized with them. He knew they were capable of better. But Nancy didn't see the difference. As long as they did the work on time and her promises were kept, she was delighted.

Barry became convinced that Nancy didn't know the difference between a great video presentation and a mediocre one. She attended all the conferences on the subject, especially if they were being held in warm places in the winter, but she didn't seem to learn anything. She came back only with descriptions of meals she had eaten while she was in New Orleans or San Diego and gossip about famous people who spoke at the conferences. On the walls of her office she had plaques and certificates from every association and course in the business, but she couldn't seem to grasp the relationship between tape speed and picture quality.

Then the company merged with another firm that didn't have an in-house audio-visual capability. Suddenly the work load in their department mushroomed. Nancy now had thirty or forty new people who could take her to lunch. She had no trouble fitting them into her schedule. But Barry and his staff could no longer keep her unreasonable promises. No matter how much they rushed, no matter how mundane they kept their work, they couldn't meet the deadlines.

Barry kept smoking more and whenever he noticed he was drinking more he told himself it wasn't that much. When Nancy started getting on his case about missed deadlines, he tried his best not to be defensive. He decided that what he had to do was educate her. He went over the process they used to get their projects done: the lead time they needed to get work back from outside labs, the problems they had scheduling time with per diem technicians, writers, and directors, all the intricacies of project management. She smiled and nodded through the whole conversation. She promised not to make rash promises and to consider the current work load before she took on new projects. Despite the staffing freeze, she would try to get Barry two more people.

Barry left the conversation with some hope that things would change for the better. That hope lasted three days. Nancy asked him to rush through yet another "exception" project. He reminded her that they already had two "emergency" jobs on top of their regular work. She admitted that she had forgotten about one of the rush projects. He told her he was going to start submitting weekly rather than monthly status reports. In this way he hoped to keep her from forgetting what was going on. He also figured that the written reports would document his predicament if he ever had to defend his performance.

Two days later, when Barry was on his way down to the word processing department to drop off his first weekly report, he ran into a manager in the actuarial department. She chided him for the condition of the storyboard he had sent her that morning. He apologized even though he thought the shoddy work was not his fault. When he got to word processing, he picked a fight with the supervisor when she told him she couldn't have his report back to him for thirty-six hours.

One of Barry's best technicians quit that afternoon. When he came in to talk to Barry about leaving, he lost his temper and blamed Barry for the chaos in the department.

Finally, Barry had to face something he had suspected all along, but wouldn't let himself think about. His people saw him as the source of the problem. He wanted to be thought of as a good boss. He wanted his people to admire him. Now an angry subordinate was quitting his job and blaming everything on him. For the first time he started to think about writing his resume. He needed to get Nancy to keep her promises. He decided to have her sign a priorities list whenever she changed her mind about something. Then, at least he could show his staff that Nancy was forcing him to shift priorities. It wasn't his fault. This decision made him feel oddly better about his position at the company.

He started to think about what the problems at work had been doing to him physically. When spring came and his summer suits didn't fit him anymore, he took a long look at himself in the mirror. He was pudgy and starting to look old. He resolved to shape up. "No matter how tired I am, I'm going out running in the morning," he promised himself and he did. He began to feel better.

The next big crisis at work came in less than a week. Nancy called from a regional meeting in Des Moines to give him another switch in priorities. "Would you mind if I put what we've said today in a memo for you to sign when you get back?"

he asked. "I don't think that's necessary" was Nancy's reply. "We've never had any trouble understanding one another." *No trouble? Barry thought. This woman has raised stupidity to an art form. How does the company expect her to manage without the benefit of a brain?* After she had hung up, he slammed down the phone.

Even though he'd been out jogging that morning, Barry went out again after work that night. *Damn, he thought as he jogged. I can't put up with her another minute.* As he rounded the corner at the Mobil station and headed for home, he started writing his resume in his head. After his shower, he started writing it with a pencil.

Barry couldn't afford to quit. He had almost no savings and didn't want to dip into the little he had, so he decided to plug along until he found another job. He knew that would take a while. But he wasn't going to let his imbecile boss push him around anymore.

When Nancy got back from Des Moines, he didn't wait for her to call him in. He went into her office with a revised schedule of his own. "This," he told her, "is a reasonable schedule for the projects we have. I'm sorry to say we will not be able to deliver on the Gordon project by the date you suggested. We are already overburdened with several rush projects, and we've just lost one of our best studio engineers."

Nancy protested. "I promised them that project. They need it by the first of July to announce the new rate structure to the agents. What good will the videotape be after the effective date of the change?"

"Well, Nancy, if we have to make this change, we have to push back one of these other projects. Which one would you suggest?"

Nancy refused to go back on any of her promises. When Barry suggested that they farm the new project out to an outside supplier, Nancy reminded him of the budget restrictions since the merger. The meeting lasted a long time. In the end, they agreed that Barry would write a report outlining the scheduling problems and his recommendations for solutions and send it to the operations vice president, Nancy's boss. Nancy wanted to stay out of the inevitable controversy.

Meanwhile, Barry got his resume to a typing and duplicating service and began to circulate it to a couple of headhunters. And he wrote his recommendation to the VP. He worked hard on it. It was his first, maybe his only chance to defeat the dummy. As he wrote it, he thought, *She's too dumb to know how dangerous it is to let me loose on her boss. She thinks the VP will blame me for not getting the work out. She thinks the only word upper management understands is yes. They can't all be that dumb.*

Barry got lucky. That last thought turned out to be right. Nancy's boss called a meeting with all three of them. Barry was nearly late for that meeting. A headhunter named John Goodman had called him ten minutes before the meeting to tell him about an interview for a great job. The encouragement he got in that phone call made him feel powerful. On his way to the meeting he realized that in the two years he had worked in her department, he had been in Lynn Gallio's office only twice. *She has always been pleasant to me, he thought. Oh, who cares, if I get in trouble with her, I'll get another job, maybe even the one John Goodman just told me about.*

Nancy was already in Lynn's office when Barry got there. She was admiring Lynn's new haircut. Her smile disappeared when Lynn started the meeting by saying that she wanted to discuss not only Barry's report, but some complaints she had been getting lately about the quality of the audio-visual department's work. Throughout the meeting, Nancy did her best to defend their work, and where she failed she blamed the problems on Barry and his staff. She also went off on a lot of tangents; time was almost up when they finally got around to discussing his recommendations.

Barry was surprised when Lynn accepted his proposal that they farm out the Gordon new rate project. She asked him to concentrate on the two projects they were doing for the training department. She told them both that the quality of their output had to improve. That was a first priority. Managers around the company were beginning to say that they could get better audio-visual service by going to the outside. She reminded Barry and Nancy how hard it was to justify the cost of their operation, especially in the current corporate atmosphere.

On the way back to their offices, Barry wondered whether that last remark was a threat or a warning. Nancy babbled about what an ambitious person Lynn was.

Barry put his mind to improving their work. He hoped the other job would come through, but he wanted to save the one he had, just in case. In fact, at one point as he sat waiting for an interview at the other company, he wrote a report on how some of their current projects could be improved. The interview went very well. And he sent the report to both Nancy and Lynn. Nancy didn't read it; she was off to another conference. Barry didn't hear anything about the report from Lynn. Then one afternoon, while Nancy was still away, he was boldly discussing his future on the telephone with John Goodman when Lynn walked up to his desk. He cut the conversation short and asked Lynn to sit down.

By the time she got up again, she had given Barry lots of encouragement about his latest report. "Your contribution here is not going unnoticed," she said. "We especially appreciate your dedication in the face of difficulties we know you are facing." The last remark was delivered with a conspiratorial look. *Could she be telling me she knows what an ignoramus Nancy is? Barry wondered. Is she promising me Nancy's job?* Barry had a lot to think about.

By the time Barry called him back, John had new information about the other job. "Great news, Barry, they want to interview you again."

When Nancy returned from Houston, Barry was too distracted to be bothered by her silly gossip and restaurant stories. He was expecting a job offer any day, and Lynn was paying more and more attention to the improvements he was making. He expected that very soon Lynn would take action. He wondered about that, *Maybe she's going to give me Nancy's job. Fantasy? Maybe, maybe not.*

The job offer from the outside came first. It was a good position. In fact, it was not unlike Nancy's. He would get more money and a chance to take charge of the audio-visual department in a big bank. But the department was smaller and the salary was not as high as Nancy's. He wondered if he should hang in and wait for Nancy's job. Then again, it was hard to resist putting his troubles behind him and starting over. He decided to talk it over with his sister Sandy, a personnel manager.

After his discussion with Sandy, Barry decided to accept the new job. His new boss was knowledgeable, could teach him new techniques, something neither Nancy nor Lynn could ever do. The money might be better if he held out for Nancy's job. But then again he might not get Nancy's job, at least not right away. This is where his sister was really helpful. She showed him how you never really make up for lost income. It would be worth giving up the bigger paycheck today for an even bigger one in the future, but only if the difference was enormous. He was sure the difference wouldn't be that great. He decided to leave.

Nancy went into shock when he handed her his resignation. She said it was totally unexpected, that she had been certain he was happy in his job. Then she started to talk about loyalty, about how good the company had been to him, and how he was taking a chance by jumping from job to job. She went on about the security of knowing that as long as you kept your nose clean you would be set for life. Barry barely listened. In the end, Nancy gave up. "I will tell Lynn about your decision," she said. "She will be very un-happy."

When Barry went to meet with Lynn, he antic-ipated that she might pressure him to stay. *What will I do, how will I feel, he wondered, when she offers me Nancy's job? I've already told John I'd take the other job. The wheels are already rolling.*

Lynn was clear about not wanting Barry to leave. She complimented his recent work and said he had a bright future with the company. Then she got that conspiratorial look on her face again. She said that changes were afoot in the company that would make him very happy. She said she couldn't tell him what the changes were but that they would make a big difference to him. "And they'll happen before very long."

"Can you tell me how long?" He was afraid to ask Lynn to be more specific about what these mysterious changes were. He assumed that he had been right all along, that they were planning on giving him Nancy's job. *At least, maybe I can find out how long I'd have to wait, he thought.*

But the most Lynn would say was, "All of the pieces are not in place yet. It's a delicate issue, and we have to be careful; but it could be just a few weeks. I can't say more."

Barry's morning jogging runs took a little longer for the next couple of days. Then he called Sandy and had lunch with her. All he did at the lunch was tell her what he had decided and why. She did what he wanted her to. She told him he had made the right decision. She said if he still had doubts, he should talk it over with their father.

"Wrong," he said. "Dad will want me to go over my options one more time. I can't do that. I've made a decision and I can't think it over again. That's the last thing I need to do."

The next day he bypassed Nancy and went straight to Lynn. He told her he appreciated her words of encouragement, but he was leaving to take the other job. "I feel it's the best thing for me right now," he said. "I learned a lot from what's happened here about how I need to conduct myself in business. But I want to learn some new things technically. I think I can do that where I'm going and I hope I won't have to face any more political hassles. For me, it's a sure thing and I have to take it." As he left Lynn's office, he felt strong enough to lift up the whole building.

When Barry left his job for a new one, he did what most people do in the face of incompetent management. And for people faced with stupid or ignorant managers, it is often the best approach. The bottom line is this: If your boss doesn't know much, he can't teach you much. If your boss is a featherbrain, your own growth in your field will be severely curtailed.

Of course, if you have to take up the slack for the boss and work at a higher level, the boss's ignorance can create more challenge for you. In such cases, your growth can be enormous—a fine arrangement provided you don't resent your boss collecting the bigger paycheck while you do two jobs.

An incompetent boss can't properly evaluate your work. I have seen bosses who had just enough information to recognize acceptable work. They knew it was okay if it looked a certain way. But when the work was a little unusual they couldn't tell whether it was unacceptable or exceptional. Often they rejected wonderful work because it didn't match their superficial idea of what was required. Their subordinates' creativity was stifled.

CAN YOU
CHANGE A DUMMY?

If a lack of intelligence is your boss's only insurmountable handicap, you can't make him smart. But there are a few constructive steps you can try to make the situation bearable.

First, check out all communications with the boss. Make sure that you understand what he is saying to you. Probe and question to verify not only what the boss has asked you to do but what the objective of the action is supposed to be. That way you will be able to head off disaster if the boss has invented some hair-brained action plan that he thinks will achieve an objective.

Give a rationale when you ask for information. Ignorant bosses are often suspicious. People fear the unknown, and ignorant people have a lot of unknowns to fear. Such fearful bosses frequently are close-mouthed. If your boss holds back information that you need, explain just how you will use it. That may make giving it to you seem less dangerous.

Try to educate the boss. Barry tried a bit of this with Nancy Ermann. In his case it didn't work very well because Nancy seemed to be stupid as well as ignorant. You can try. It may work. Some bosses are actually willing to learn from their subordinates.

Tap whatever resources your boss does have. Your annoyance with your boss may stem from his ignorance in one area. Recognizing his expertise in other subjects will allow you to respect him. It may keep down your frustration level.

Eventually, with the truly numbskulled, you will decide to go elsewhere. Like Barry you will probably have to stick around where you are until you find another job. Here are some ways you can maintain your sanity until you find a better spot.

Find a reliable way of getting information from and to the boss. Try Barry's approach of frequent written reports. Getting the boss to sign off on work plans and priority lists may work. If you're not sure your boss knows how to read, you might try instituting a series of regular meetings at which you can discuss important matters. You might want to document these meetings. Don't fill the files up with a lot of unnecessary paper. But if they'll serve your purposes later, write your "CYA" memos.

Use all the leeway you have in how and what you do on the job. For your own satisfaction and to earn your pay, make yourself as effective as you can. This approach will also help you if you transfer to another job in the company rather than going outside.

In fact, whatever happens you will want to get as much recognition as you can from managers other than your boss. In the end, Barry had an option to stay where he was and wait for the mystery job Lynn alluded to. He decided not to exercise that option, but if Lynn hadn't noticed his competence, he wouldn't have had the choice at all. You may find that competent people around you can help you find another job or give you a reference. At the very least their admiration will help you maintain your self-confidence. That is vital.

6

DEVILS, SCOUNDRELS, LIARS, THIEVES, AND SNAKES IN THE GRASS

It is as if People were half horrible and half nice. Perhaps they are even more than half horrible, and when they are left to themselves they run wild.

T. H. White
The Once and Future King

H

ave you ever felt as if you've entered the twilight zone? I spent a morning there once. I was driving to a meeting at a client company when I heard on the radio that several managers of the company I was about to visit were being indicted in a product liability case. They manufactured camping equipment which would be used by children. The indictment stated that the company had failed to fireproof the equipment. The prosecution had copies of memos indicating that the fireproofing would have cost one dollar per item. The managers of the department, with the approval of their top management, had decided to forgo the fireproofing as a cost-saving technique. As a result, two young boys burned to death and one was severely disfigured.

The appalling story made me question whether I should even be doing business with a company that increased its profits by cutting such corners. I proceeded to the meeting not knowing what my next move would be.

When I got to the company the strangest thing happened. Nobody said anything about the indictments; people looked blank and evaded my questions. Everyone from managers to the receptionist seemed intent on ignoring the news that their bosses were suspected criminals with very strong evidence against them. It was business as usual. How could those people just ignore what was going on? Why do people continue to work for dishonest bosses who are endangering or defrauding the public?

I guess it's human nature to think the best of our close associates. Whenever a sniper climbs up in a high place and randomly kills several people, his neighbors always say what a sweet, quiet person he was. We don't want to think ill of others. We like to think we are all humane as well as human. It breaks my heart to have to say it isn't true.

Some bosses are purely despicable. They lie, steal, take or give bribes. They engage in insider trading, make and sell dangerous products, use dishonest accounting practices, and fix prices. They use the route of the midnight requisition to get the power or wealth they crave. In the newspapers and in the privacy of our offices and factories, we observe that some business people are scoundrels who value only themselves and their own aggrandizement. Often these days we see managers explaining their actions purely on the basis of performance. Values and human decency don't seem to figure in their equations.

But regardless of what others are doing, you must guard yourself against falling into the prevailing moral turpitude. Live your business life by your values. Ultimately that is how you will be judged by your fellow human beings (and, some believe, by your Creator).

Of course, the majority of business people conduct their business ethically. They are upstanding people who follow a fully functioning conscience. But if you work for a thief and a liar, the fact that most business people are moral is no consolation to you. You feel disgusted, betrayed, dirty by association.

The worst snakes in the grass are extraordinarily dedicated to their nefarious goals. They communicate a great focus of commitment. Ordinarily, managers' dedication is a powerful attraction. We are drawn to them by their devotion to a cause or an idea that also attracts us. With some bosses, however, we find out later that their dedication is sick, that they are willing to use immoral means to achieve their ends. The power they amass creates even more of the arrogance and insecurity that fuels their diseased ambition. They will break the law, or they will invent vile and underhanded tactics against which no law has yet been passed. They disregard the safety and well-being of others to serve their own ends and gratify their egos. We have to stop them. We have to stop ourselves from cooperating in their wrong-headed and wrong-hearted schemes.

A few lawbreaking employers do actually wind up in jail. Three executives of a silver recycling plant each got twenty-five years in prison and $10,000 fines when they were convicted after one of their employees died from inhaling cyanide fumes on the job. The sentencing judge said the defendants were clearly aware of the dangers posed to their employees by the working conditions they created but did nothing to alleviate the dangers or to warn the employees that their lives were at stake. The employers were eventually brought to justice, but only after the employee was dead. The case was believed to be the first in the history of the United States where employers were found guilty of murder after an employee died of job-related causes.

The law seeks to protect employees from companies that cut corners at the expense of employee safety. Criminal managers are sometimes uncovered and prosecuted. But employees need to look to their own protection—the protection of their bodies and their integrity—in the face of villianous management.

LEARN TO RECOGNIZE THE POISONOUS ONES

Be prepared to guard yourself against bosses who have lost their ability to distinguish right from wrong. Watch for the telltale behaviors of immoral or amoral management. First, they start to block out information that contradicts what they want to hear. They become so drunk with ego gratification that like real drunks they lose their judgment. The bottom line becomes their measure of self-esteem. To add dollars to operating profits, they cut corners on products that will later endanger the lives of children.

Not all snakes in the grass are overt criminals. Sometimes their dastardly deeds are subtle. The damage they do is silent. Like Norma Teller's former boss. She'll never go to jail, but she's committed a number of unindictable offenses. Her name is Laura Blasko, but she insisted everyone call her Doctor Blasko. She never said what she meant, and she never gave anyone a straight answer. She used her credentials as a psychologist to get herself a job running the counseling and outplacement department of a major financial institution. She presented an accepting, Mother Earth image. She did people favors, bolstered their egos, sympathized with their positions, and got them to tell her things.

Employees with problems flocked to her. She kept hot coffee, a box of tissues, and a warm smile handy at all times. She had a cartoon hanging on the outside of her office door showing Lucy of "Peanuts" behind her booth—you know, the one that says, "Psychiatric Help 5 cents. The Doctor Is In."

Norma admired the way Dr. Blasko helped everyone who came to her. She always made time for people, even though she had a full schedule. Norma knew exactly how busy Dr. Blasko was. As Dr. Blasko's secretary, Norma kept her calendar, answered her phone, and typed her reports. Dr. Blasko lectured Norma frequently on the importance of keeping the files confidential. She reminded Norma that they both had access to highly sensitive information about many people.

When it came time for her performance appraisal, Norma was, for the first time, not the least bit apprehensive. She was sure Dr. Blasko would be sympathetic. And she was.

She began the conversation by asking Norma,

as she always did, "How's the baby?" Norma had just returned from maternity leave; Norma's daughter was just four months old.

"Oh, she's great, Dr. Blasko. She smiles and sits up. She's like a real person."

"Tell me, Norma, how you feel about being a working mother?" Dr. Blasko said, pouring a little more coffee into Norma's cup.

"I feel okay about it. The only time I worry about the baby is when I'm on my way home from work. Sometimes between the train station and my apartment, I start to think that something awful has happened to her. I can't wait to get there to make sure she's okay."

Dr. Blasko gave Norma a great performance appraisal. Norma knew she was doing a good job and was glad it was noticed. The work went along and everything seemed fine. Then Norma saw her dream job posted—secretary in the office of the chairman. Norma's friend Charlie Lystein was the chairman's administrative assistant. They set up an interview for Norma, certain that she was the strongest candidate. Even before the interview, they were already planning the projects they would do together.

After the interview, Dr. Blasko asked Norma how it went. "Great," said Norma. "I think I'm going to get it. My only regret will be leaving here. I've really enjoyed working with you."

When the news came that Norma wasn't going to get the job, she was shocked. Dr. Blasko consoled her. "Oh, Norma, what a shame. We were all so sure you would get the job."

When Charlie called Norma to have lunch, Norma figured he wanted to console her. But when they met, he was angry. He handed her a piece of paper. "You can't tell anybody I showed you this," he said, "but I thought you should know what a slime you work for. That's the chairman's handwriting."

What Charlie handed Norma was her job posting application and on the back was written, "Blasko = N tremendous guilt feelings about working with baby. Insecure about femininity. Potentially unstable. Bad risk." It took Norma a minute to figure out the chairman's handwriting. She looked up at Charlie. "Does this mean . . ."

"That your boss gave you a bad recommendation," Charlie said, taking the paper away. "What did you say to her to draw her to such a conclusion? You've got to stop trusting people with personal information."

Norma was shocked at first. She didn't want to believe what had happened. Then she started to notice little things that made her suspicious. Dr. Blasko's smile came and went so quickly. People would come out of Dr. Blasko's office and tell Norma what Blasko had said or what she had promised to do. But then, when Norma got the notes to type up, the file papers said something completely different. Blasko promised to meet with management to resolve employees' problems. Those meetings seldom took place.

Norma never confronted Blasko. She just kept her head low until she got another job. About ten months later at a party Norma met the spouse of one of her husband's colleagues. The man was a professor at a nearby university. Norma said, "An old boss of mine had a Ph.D. in industrial psychology from Wesleyan."

"You must be mistaken," he said. "Wesleyan doesn't award Ph.D.s in industrial psych." Norma knew she wasn't mistaken. She had typed Blasko's credentials many times. She figured this man she had just met, with the patronizing air, must be mistaken himself. Then it hit her what had really happened.

She called Charlie the following Monday. He took care of the rest. Once the company discovered Blasko's Ph.D. was a phony, she was fired.

Can you trust your boss? Will he turn on you and betray your trust? Will she give you a direct order and, if it turns out to be the wrong thing to do, later throw you to the lions? Will he tell you the truth? The whole truth? Will you get nothing but evasions and vague responses to your concerns?

Not all secretive bosses are reprobates, but be suspicious of bosses who seem to conceal things unnecessarily. The truth spoken plainly may be difficult to deal with, but up-front and explicit information is seldom really harmful. If your boss is covert in his actions, and especially if you are asked to be furtive in yours, make sure you know why the secrecy is necessary.

If your boss owns the company, he has a right to keep the corporate results a secret. However, unnecessary mystery about how the company is doing can be a sign of dirty dealings. Executives will not want anyone to see the books while they're stealing the corporate assets.

Watch out for bosses who are constantly protesting their honesty and conversely for those who are always suspicious that other people are trying to steal things or put something over on them. Not everyone who sees a thief around every corner is a thief himself, but most honest people are also somewhat trusting. They don't go around saying, "I am not a crook."

Beware of the consummate corporate politician. Politicking takes many forms. Bosses in this category, for instance, will look for powerful allies and scorn those whose friendship has become a liability. They don't give of themselves; they look to scratch the backs of people who can exchange the favor.

EVIL MANAGERS
POISON PRODUCTIVITY
AND PROFITS

Most managers shepherd the organizations in their charge and do their best to keep them healthy. Some make legitimate mistakes that cause disaster. Inept bosses may be dangerous but they are seldom evil. There are a few bosses, however, who purposely push the organization into the ground. They raid the corporate coffers and walk away with their pockets full while the employees are left with very little, sometimes without even a company to work for. One company filed for bankruptcy only four months after its five top officers awarded themselves bonuses of $25,000 each. We've all read in the papers how auto executives raked in millions of dollars in bonuses while the workers on the assembly line were being asked to give up raises and benefits.

Serious managers consider the impact of such decisions on the morale and productivity of their employees. They realize they cannot expect workers to be loyal if the people in charge are filling their own wallets and disregarding the company's future.

The government is beginning to crack down on some of the worst cases. They are calling into question the lucrative severance agreements that serve no business purpose except to ensure the future wealth of current management.

Some financial abuses, like insider trading, are illegal, but many of the cleverest modern executive thieves are not breaking any laws. Their stratagems are perfectly legal—the leveraged buyout, hostile takeovers, and defenses against unwanted acquisitions. To achieve or maintain power in the corporation, they run up enormous corporate debt. To service the debt, assets have to be sold off, companies have to be restructured, payrolls have to be cut. Cash ordinarily invested in expansion and R and D is used to pay off loans. Pay raises shrink and jobs disappear. Employees wind up working for companies whose future is far less secure.

These practices have been called the "casino economy," an apt title since a few win and many lose. They have enormous potential for economic chaos, especially if the economy weakens. But the management of your company may be seduced into playing fast and loose with the corporate assets and betraying the employees. They may be blinded by the huge personal profits of doing deals—dirty or otherwise.

If your boss uses base methods to achieve her ends, you may feel guilty by association even if you don't profit from her shenanigans. If you work for a snake in the grass, others may equate you with her. Your reputation as well as your self-respect may be at stake. If your boss can pin the bad behavior on you, you may even risk going to jail.

Even if you don't go up the river, you probably won't go up the ladder, either. Foul bosses stunt the careers of their employees. They prove their superiority by showing others that they are the only ones who can get ahead. They hang on to hardworking employees at the expense of the employee's own advancement. They make sure their people have little or no exposure to others in the company. If another manager becomes interested in someone, they badmouth the employee to make sure no one else wants him. They rob their people of self-confidence to prevent them from seeking success elsewhere. Vile.

If you want to hear about vile, talk to someone whose boss takes credit away from him. Perhaps it's happened to you. You suggest some improvement in the way the work is done and the next thing you know your idea is being sent to top management in a memo signed by your boss with no mention of you. As Charlie Brown would say,

"Aarrrgh!" The logical extension of this behavior is for the boss to make sure that although he gets credit for your accomplishments, only you get blamed for your mistakes. "AARRRGGHHH!!"

Where immoral bosses are in power, people start to guard what they say and restrict what they do. Productivity and innovation suffer from the lack of cooperation and information exchange. Hostility and suspicion reign.

Even if you are not the direct victim of a scoundrel boss, once you know your boss has no morals you know you can be next. The conflict between the way you have to live at work and your values leads to great internal stress. Eventually you begin to mistrust everything the boss says or does. Your position becomes intolerable. That's what happened to Barbara Sansone when she got a new boss.

Barbara had worked for twelve years in the corporate communications department of a pharmaceutical company. When Chris Schmitt arrived to take over the department, Barbara was head of employee communications, the group that published the weekly employee newspaper and a quarterly employee magazine. Because she had such a high visibility job, Barbara knew hundreds of people in the company, including all of the members of the executive committee. People liked her and her work. In planning the company newspaper, she tried to keep a good balance between news of weddings, births, and service anniversaries and "hard" news about profits, new products, reorganizations, and the like. She loved her job and, unlike her colleague Earl Meyers, who managed the public relations effort, she had no resentment about Chris being brought in from the outside to manage the department.

Barbara never expected any serious changes in what she was doing. But from day one, Chris seemed to have it in for her. He immediately announced what he saw as his mission: the modernization of the department. "Management," he said at that first staff meeting, "has brought me in here to make this the kind of corporate communications department that can serve the future of this company, not its past. I'm putting you all on notice that what you are doing now is automatically suspect. We are going to bring this place into the twenty-first century, even before the twentieth century ends."

No one in the department was quite sure what that meant, but they were sure they would find out soon enough. Barbara thought it couldn't mean much about what she was doing. *Newspapers always have to cover the same things, she thought, and her people were already using state-of-the-art methods. What could Chris's ultimatum mean to me? she wondered.*

Chris soon asked her to conduct a survey to determine how her group's efforts could better serve the corporation's needs. She told him that she had recently done such a study and gave him a copy of the final report. She turned proudly to the attachments and showed him a memo written by the chairman complimenting the quality of both the newspaper and the magazine. She fully expected that to be the end of that. It was not.

Chris asked to see all the copy for the ensuing issues of both publications. He criticized her choice of a theme for the Christmas issue as trite. He told her that employees were not as interested in seeing their names and pictures in print as she imagined.

Chris's next move puzzled Barbara at first. He asked her to do a cost and quality evaluation comparing their present printer with one in another state. She protested that working with a local printer was much more efficient than working with someone so far away. "Frequently, we have to go to the printer to check proofs when we have to make last-minute changes," she said. "We'll run into real problems if our printer is a plane ride—not a few minutes' drive—away."

Chris insisted and Barbara complied. Her study showed that the cost was a little lower with the new printer, but quality was about equal. In her final recommendation, she included convenience as a factor and concluded that despite the small savings, they would be better staying with the nearby printer.

"That's what I mean about moving into the future," Chris said. "This company may have been a country club for years, but these are hardheaded times. If you can't be profit-minded, you have no business working in a profit-making organization." At Chris's insistence, they switched to the other printer.

Barbara's friend Paul Greco asked her why the choice had to be between those two printers. "There are printers all over the place. If a lower price is what he wanted, why didn't he have you survey several other printers in this area. What's so special about this printer in Cincinnati?"

Barbara's mind stopped. Why hadn't that thought occurred to her before it was too late? "I wish I had thought about that," she said. "We've already signed a contract with the new printer. We can't change now. I've been so busy trying to look competent and cooperative lately, I seem to be losing my strategic brain cells."

Paul's question haunted Barbara. Why the printer in Cincinnati? "Chris has an ulterior motive," she thought. The idea of a kickback entered her mind fleetingly one morning when she was drying her hair. She dismissed it. *You are imagining things because you don't like him and he threatens you, she told herself. He's difficult, but that doesn't make him a thief.*

Then, on the first Friday in May, Barbara got a call saying that the spring issue of the magazine weighed more than usual. The mailing room needed authorization to spend extra money on postage. Chris had strictly forbidden her and Earl to authorize over-budget expenses without his approval and Chris wasn't in the office that day. She got his number and called him at home. A housekeeper answered and told her that Mr. and Mrs. Schmitt had already left for the weekend; gratuitously she added that they had gone to Mrs.

Schmitt's niece's wedding in Cincinnati. Barbara had to go to Chris's boss for authorization of the extra expense.

Then she called her friend Paul. Over a beer after work that evening, she told Paul about her suspicions about the printer and how she couldn't get it out of her head that Chris was getting kickbacks. She thought she should do something about it, but she wasn't sure what she could do. "At the very least," she said, "he's probably giving the business to his wife's relatives. I'd like to let him know that I know."

"But you don't know, not for sure," Paul said. "I would be careful. He's slick; he isn't going to be easy to deal with." Paul reminded her that she liked her job and warned her that Chris could move against her if she threatened him.

"I do love my job; at least I used to before he came along. I don't think it would be that easy to get another job like it, not this close to home anyway. I'd better see if I can't make the best of the situation. It frosts me, though. My people and I are inconvenienced by having the printer 850 miles away. Even though the printing bill is a little lower it really costs the company more when you consider the phone calls, the Federal Express charges, the delays. And he goes around getting credit for modernizing the place. If this is modernization, I want to be old-fashioned."

Barbara decided to say something innocuous and see how Chris would react. On Monday when she went into Chris's office to review that week's copy for the newspaper, she told him she had called him at home. In as lighthearted a tone as she could muster, she said, "You should have told me you were going to Cincinnati. I could have given you the galleys to bring to the printer." She watched his eyes and he looked into hers. She saw a look of recognition. She was more convinced than ever that Chris was up to something at least slightly dishonest.

For the next couple of months, Barbara did her job and tried to steer clear of Chris. It was easier than she thought because he was busy finding a new head of public relations—Earl Meyers had quit. Earl's last words to Barbara were "I won't work for that snake." He refused to explain. Everyone in the department thought it was just sour grapes because Earl had expected to get Chris's job. They all knew he had been upset since Chris was hired. Barbara hoped they were right. But she wondered if Earl had suspected something, too.

The winner in the public relations manager hunt turned out not to be Earl's assistant manager, Bob Montgomery, as everyone hoped. Chris brought in someone from the outside, a former associate. People in the department were disappointed. Barbara's suspicions grew.

"These people scare me, Paul," she told her friend over lunch one day. "And this Larry Wallace, who took Earl's place, is a super sleaze. He calls me 'Babe.' I can't bear it. And Chris has given him a company car to use while he gets settled. He moved here from a hundred miles away, for heaven's sake. What are we talking about, 'until he gets settled'? The two of them are constantly taking each other to lunch. I know they're using company expense accounts. And Larry keeps bragging about how he can help me if I have a problem at the printer's. I know they're up to no good." All Paul could do was try to calm Barbara down and remind her that she had decided to make the best of the situation.

The following week Chris asked Barbara to run a feature article in the paper about Larry. "I think it would be a good idea for us to introduce our new public relations manager to the company. Put it into the paper for the week after next."

Barbara objected. "We've always made it a policy not to blow our own horns here," she said. "Besides, we already have a feature for that issue about the new flexible benefit plan. We can't take that out." The meeting went on for an hour. Despite Barbara's arguments, Chris insisted on the article about Larry. In the end, he questioned her professionalism and her loyalty. "I'm loyal to the company and my own values," she finally burst out. "I have no loyalty to you and your cronies." Barbara was shocked herself at her outburst. She was even more surprised that Chris reneged. "Forget the feature article for now. We'll work this out some other way," he said.

A few days later, Chris told Barbara she would be in charge of arranging the company picnic and organizing the United Way campaign. She reminded him that she was already stretched to get all her work done. She protested at having two special projects over the next few months, especially since she would be shorthanded during the vacation season. "I'm giving you a direct order," he said. "There isn't anyone else here who can do these jobs. Just do your best; I'm sure you'll do all right."

Barbara was sure he was trying to set her up to fail. He could try, but she would fight back. She went into high gear, marshaled all her resources, and called on her friends in the organization who owed her favors. Eventually she got everything done. In the end, despite a small drop in the quality of the newspaper, she felt as if she'd won.

At performance appraisal time Chris dropped the bombshell. Barbara's appraisal was mediocre. For the first time since she came to the company, she wasn't getting a raise. He cited problems with the newspaper and told her her attitude wasn't professional. He wrote on the appraisal form that she was uncooperative. And she had to sign it. She refused.

Paul advised her to give up and look for another job. "This is driving you nuts," he said. "It's been a good job for years, but it's time for you to move on. Go somewhere where you will be appreciated. The odds are against you here, that's for sure."

"I won't. I'm not going to be pushed out by him so he can bring another one of his vassals in here to help him steal from the company." There was fight in her voice, but there were tears in her eyes.

Chris didn't give Barbara time to garner her resources. The very next day he told her he was bringing in an "independent" firm to make an "objective" analysis of the quality of her group's work. "I expect you to give them your full cooperation," he said. "Anything less will be grounds for me to take action against you."

Barbara had worried for some time that her job might be in jeopardy, but now she had heard it right from Chris's mouth. She decided that her one objective over the next few weeks was to make sure he didn't take her job away from her. At the meeting with the outside firm to plan the evaluation, she was collaboration personified. "Maybe," she thought, "the fix is already in against me, but if there's any room to maneuver, I'm going to get a fair analysis from the consultants." She said nothing more to Chris about her suspicions or his behavior. She did, however, get as close as possible to the consultant who was doing the evaluation.

One day, about midway through the evaluation process, Barbara called up the consultant and told her that she suspected that Chris was going to use the evaluation to force her out of her job. Barbara knew she was taking a risk. But she figured that if the consultant was honest, she might take Barbara's side. If the fix was already in and the consultant was in cahoots with Chris, the consultant would tell him that Barbara knew what they were up to. Either way, taking the consultant into her confidence would serve Barbara's purpose.

The consultant assured Barbara that she would be objective. Since Barbara couldn't be sure, she played her ace in the hole. She went to talk to Mike Levelle, the administrative vice president. He was Chris's boss, and she was going over Chris's head but she had known Mike for years. She didn't tell him about her suspicions about the kickbacks, and she didn't even ask him if he knew about Chris's expense account abuses. All she told him were the facts about her assignments, her performance evaluation, and Chris's threats. "Mike, I hate to put you on the spot," she said. "I know you can't reveal anything to me and I don't want you to. All I ask you to do is look into what he's doing and the decisions he makes. He doesn't know I've come to you, and I don't expect you to make any special exceptions for me. I'll just go back to my desk and try to keep out of his way."

After that meeting with Mike, everything seemed to stop. Months went by and nothing happened. She knew the consultant had finished her report, but Barbara never saw a copy of it. She thought about asking Chris if she could see it, but she decided against opening the subject. She felt as if she were in limbo. Then, shortly after the first of the year, Larry suddenly left the company. Less than two weeks later, Chris said he would be leaving as soon as they found a replacement for him. He said he and Larry were going to go into business for themselves.

Barbara never knew what happened behind the scenes. Privately she and Paul speculated about why Chris left so abruptly, but they never found out for sure. As is frequently the case with dishonest employees, no charges were brought, no announcements were made.

Two years later, when Mike Levelle retired, she did a special feature on him and his contribution to the company. He was very touched by the tribute. He sent her a bouquet of flowers and a note that said, "Thank you to a person who really cares."

If you view Barbara's story from her perspective, you see that despite some difficulty she triumphed in the end over a thief and a liar. She is a hero because she not only saved her own job, she saved the company from a crook. On the other hand, you can read the story and see her as a paranoid person who was unnecessarily suspicious, who repressed her own jealousy, and who was really the perpetrator, not the victim. She never had proof that Chris was taking kickbacks or that he was padding his expense accounts. And that's the difficulty in combating a snake in the grass. If your boss is at all good at the game you'll never find the "smoking gun." And without that, your motives may be suspect. Upper management may not see events from your point of view. You could come out of such a situation with your conscience, but not your job, intact. You have to decide what to do and how to do it. Your moral choices are your own to make. But you have to live with yourself and that may be difficult if your basic integrity and principles are compromised on the job.

First, carefully evaluate the alternatives, not only yours, but theirs. Resist the age-old advice to fight fire with fire. If you combat the boss's subterfuges with your own dirty tricks, you will become tacky yourself. Playing their game by their rules means turning into one of them.

Try to influence the boss or the decision-making process whenever you suspect moral issues are being ignored. Pose the questions that will direct attention to ethics. Your attempts may be ignored, but at least you will have tried to push things in the moral direction. Sometimes, if the company has an established value system, you can use it. Recently, a woman I know was being forced to take early retirement. Her boss was trying to push her out because her self-confidence and long experience with the company made it difficult for him to push her around. Several managers she had worked with over the years put pressure on her boss. "This is not the way we do things around here," was their objection. "This is not a company where we force people out of their jobs after years of good service. If her performance is not up to snuff, say so. Otherwise leave her alone." When enough people had invoked the established value system of the company, the manager had to back down.

Stand up against managers who disregard honesty, ethics, and humanity. Principle dictates that you do this. Playing helpless won't work in the long run. "I was just following orders" went out as a viable excuse after World War II, thank goodness.

Beware of temptation. Your immoral boss may ask you to jump on the wayward wagon. You may be enticed with money, status, or power, all of which can blur the ethics of an action. The boss's power may also confuse you. In trying to make you comply with nefarious requests, she may appeal to your "objectivity" or your "team spirit."

I have seen a couple of people who were corrupted by the roles they were asked to play. Both were brilliant young men who were adopted by powerful mentors who sought to use them and promised to reward them. They were both put to work as hatchet men, sent into areas of the organization to fire people or act as front men for bosses who didn't want to be identified with an unpopular operation.

Jim Bellamy admired his tough guy department head in the marketing department of the automobile company where he worked. His boss repeatedly put him in charge of problem areas and encouraged him to work fast to put things on track. Often at the boss's suggestion, and always with his approval, Jim used brutal methods. He bullied people in public, fired people left and right, and browbeat them into submission. Soon, fear preceded Jim's arrival in any new assignment. After a while, even if he wanted to change his style, he would have had difficulty. People would think the "new Jim" was just another one of his stratagems. Experience had taught everyone that he was a cold-blooded executioner. They related to him with fear and suspicion. Jim's been lucky so far. His mentor remains in power, and he still has a job. But they preside over a less and less successful organization. If you talk to other people in the industry, all of the best people have already left the organization. The interesting thing is that people hate Jim, not his boss who is the real demon.

Matt Holler was not so lucky. Another wunderkind who was adopted by a powerful senior manager, he too was cast in the role of grim reaper. In this case, the senior manager was Matt's boss's boss, who needed to orchestrate a staff reduction. He gave the assignment to Matt, but the senior man laid down the rules. After months of behind the scenes work, the organization fired sixty middle managers in three days. We all realize that from time to time organizations must let people go. The objection to Matt's project was not to its ends, but to his means. A list was drawn up of those marked for what we in business, with remarkable candor, call termination. One by one the "chosen" were called into their bosses' offices, given the bad news, and sent directly to an outplacement firm for processing. They were forbidden to return to their desks, even to call their families and say good-bye to their coworkers. Managers all over the company did the dirty deeds, but Matt was known as the architect of the effort. More than ten years later, long-term employees are still calling those three days Mean Matt Holler's Hell Days. Matt never recovered his reputation. Eventually, he left the company. He started a restaurant that lasted less than a year. Then he went and tried to find a job like the one he had, but word had gone out in the business community. Matt couldn't get a job within the industry. Two and a half years after he left his last job he was still looking, even trying other parts of the country. But he was drinking more and more and had a hard time staying organized and on his toes. Eventually the alcoholism took over. Not even his friends who stood by him in the dark days right after the purge know where he is now.

Perhaps Matt's alcoholism was genetic. It may have gotten him sooner or later anyway. But maybe the loss of self-esteem he suffered after the purge pushed him over the edge. If you let your boss cast you in a role you abhor, you may find that others abhor you. They will judge you by your actions regardless of who gave you the order. Eventually, everyone will relate to you as the person you have been pretending to be. You will find it nearly impossible to jettison the role. You will be trapped by your past actions.

DEALING WITH THE DASTARDLY

How do you avoid being snared into bad behavior by a corrupt boss? What can you do when your boss orders you to do something you know you shouldn't? More difficult still, how can you avoid courses of action that don't look all that bad until you are in the middle of them and it's too late?

First, be careful of too much objectivity. If your gut reaction to something is negative, don't dismiss those feelings too soon. Suffer the discomfort and analyze the issue. Identify the source of your consternation. The pain of soul-searching at the beginning may be far less than the remorse later on.

Avoid mentally abdicating responsibility. When you hear yourself think *he's the boss, it's his responsibility* or *she wouldn't ask me to do anything wrong* an alarm should go off in your head. These thoughts are the basis for a lot of self-deception.

Don't overreact to your suspicions before you have proof. Grandstand plays in which you prematurely expose the boss's vices and transgressions may backfire on you. Think back to Barbara's story earlier in this chapter. Suppose she had made a public declaration of her suspicions when they first surfaced. Despite her good record with the company, top management could have labeled her a nut-case as easily as a hero.

Look to your own power. The boss needs your cooperation to do her job effectively. She can be severely hurt if you refuse to cooperate. I don't mean that you need to threaten her. Just draw the line on what you will do and what you won't do. True, you may risk being tossed out on your ear. But if she fires you, your boss will have no way of controlling what you do with what you know about her shenanigans. Besides, sometimes finding a new job is less trouble than trying to keep the one you have.

If you suspect the boss's motives, question them. Use your supportive techniques as outlined in chapter four. Don't shoot with both barrels, but test your assumptions. Watch the boss's behavior for clues about what underlies his actions.

Call the game. Tacky behavior is more comfortable if no one seems to be noticing it. Sometimes people delude themselves that they are fooling all of the people all of the time. But they give up their tricks if someone calls attention to them. This tactic may work even if you seem to be joking when you mention your suspicions. You might say something like, "Gee, Howie, if I didn't know you so well, I might think you were trying to steal my idea." It might work. At the very least it will tell the boss that his slip is showing.

Document. If you are afraid your boss will steal your suggestions, put them in writing before you discuss them. I once had a boss who was such an idea-robber that whenever I sent him a recommendation I had to send a copy to his boss. It didn't endear me to my boss at all, but I wasn't trying to win a popularity contest with him. Who wants to be loved by a snake?

YOU MAY HAVE TO GO

If your boss's misdeeds are unbearable, you may decide to find a place where you can work without feeling dirty. It may be best to escape before you are called upon to testify at the trial. While you are waiting to find another job, draw a line in your mind around what you are unwilling to do and don't cross it. Try to see the experience as a test you have to pass. You need to take your self-esteem with you when you leave. Concentrate on what you're learning about people, and especially about yourself. Keep a low profile and move as quickly as you can.

If your boss is breaking the law, report him to the authorities.

SEXUAL HARASSMENT

A special case reptilian boss is the one who demands sexual favors. The U.S. government, the Working Woman Institute and *Redbook* magazine have all conducted studies that show millions of employees have experienced sexual harassment. As a result, they suffer from headaches, depression, ulcers, and high blood pressure. If they refuse their boss's attentions, they are denied raises and promotions, and sometimes they lose their jobs. Some bosses tell their employees off-color jokes, make suggestive remarks, or brush up against them "accidentally." Others make more serious and overt demands and threats. Experts say it is best to take action immediately to stop any form of sexual harassment. Here's what to do.

First, tell the boss to stop. Be direct and clear. Some people use humor to put the boss off. Sometimes it works. But you may give your boss the impression that you think his antics are funny. I think it's best to make your objections serious. Tell him just what it is that you dislike. "Steve, I don't want you to touch me. Please don't do it any more." Or "Chris, you may find those stories amusing, but I find them embarrassing. Please don't tell them in front of me."

If step one doesn't work, write the boss a note. Again be straightforward. Talk about the future, not the past. It isn't necessary at this point to document what the boss has done to offend you, but you should be clear about what you don't want to happen in the future. Send the memo only to the boss, but keep a copy.

If the brat persists, keep a log of what he does. Include the action, your response, the date, time, and place. At the same time, start documenting your work performance. Sleazy bosses often fight back by attacking the quality of your work. You want to have your defenses ready.

Enlist the support of others. If you suspect your coworkers are experiencing the same problem, you may want to get them to adopt the same procedures. That way if your evidence is questioned, you have others who can corroborate your story.

Go to the personnel department or your boss's boss with your grievance. This will be your last effort to rectify the situation before you take legal action. If they don't help you, you will have no choice but to sue the boss.

If a lawsuit seems the only way to get justice, then seek out a service agency or use your state or city antidiscrimination agency to help you. Ultimately the law is there to protect you from intimidating or offensive sexual behavior on the part of the boss. You don't have to suffer, you don't have to remain silent, and you don't have to sacrifice your career to your virtue or your virtue to your career.

7

SLAVE DRIVERS, BULLIES, TYRANTS, AND DICTATORS

*How Shild made slaves of
soldiers from every Land,
crowds of captives he'd
beaten into terror.*

Beowulf

B

osses in this category believe in the law of supply and demand: you supply, they demand. They use dirty tricks and tacky tactics to get you to do their bidding. They overwork you and begrudge you your rewards. This is the modern vestige of the management style of the foremen who worked on the pyramids. It continued as the dominant (!) management style in the Industrial Revolution, and there are still a lot of these unbearable bosses around. You are bound to run into one at some point.

Once you are in their employ, they are easy to identify. The problem is how to deal with them. Short of reporting them to Amnesty International, your best bet is to understand their motivation and their nasty tactics and to have a few strategies of your own for dealing with them.

WHY DO BOSSES BULLY PEOPLE?

Lots of forces can turn an ordinary person into a corporate despot. Many tyrants merely make unrealistic assumptions about the nature of their job. Cal Cambridge worked for a large public relations firm. He had to beat out a lot of competition to become his own worst enemy. A former Olympic ice hockey player, he was full of energy and great with clients, exuding a self-confidence that inspired their faith in the firm. Cal's tough-guy attitude seemed to match the macho image of the firm and its board of directors. He rose quickly, but throughout his career his big-man-on-campus attitude never changed. His favorites, known to the disgruntled in the firm as Cal's pals, moved forward with him. Like a clique of top jocks, they went around oblivious to or disdainful of the talented but less egotistical staff on whom the success of the firm depended.

Cal's appointment as president signaled the staff that his aggressive way with people would permeate the firm. His superior attitude and smart-aleck management style fostered jealousy and divisiveness. Everyone kept busy—some trying to impress Cal so they could snag favored assignments, others moaning about their lack of status in the firm, and quite a few writing their resumes. The work suffered. The firm became less and less likely to fulfill Cal's promises to the clients. They lost several pieces of business.

Cal, blindsided by a lifetime of success as a charging bull, was unable to figure out what his demoralized staff needed to reunite and inspire it. He decided to take an action guaranteed to exacerbate the problem. At a meeting called to discuss strategies for dealing with falling revenues, he announced his management approach—the credo of bullies everywhere. "It's time," he said, "to kick ass and take names."

Cal's actions, which aggravated the morale problems and led to even higher turnover and further loss of business, were based on his negative attitudes about people. Good bosses see people as competent and willing to work. They draw on their people's inner desire to do a good job and feel satisfied with what they have done. Slave drivers see people as lazy and unmotivated. They coerce and manipulate because they see such actions as the only way to get the work done. Research into managerial styles shows that only one out of five bosses is optimistic about people. The other four have the low expectations that lead them to pressure their employees.

Often autocrats believe the only way to succeed is at someone else's expense. They drive their people so they can look important and feel in control. Sometimes oppressive bosses are overachievers who set unrealistic standards for themselves as well as for other people. The superambitious often expect their subordinates to share their neurotic perfectionism.

Bullies are basically insecure. I'm not asking you to feel sorry for them or to put up with their atrocities. Just figure them out so you can take some control over the situation. Your dictator boss may be a former colleague who now treats you like an underling because he doesn't really feel worthy to lead you. Denigrating you may make him feel better. He may be so intent on gaining security and feeling in control that he can't see his own tactlessness. Never mind that the tyrant's techniques are inefficient—these bosses never allow themselves to be distracted by the truth. All they want is to comfort themselves by feeling powerful. If the dictator is a woman she may be overcompensating for her "femininity" by turning hard.

The power-hungry who are frustrated will often demean their employees as a way of bolstering their own sagging self-image. And these bullies pick their victims from among the vulnerable—people who lack power or self-confidence. Roberta Metzger ran the accounting office in a university. Her subordinates included a couple of supervisors and seven clerks. She stood over them while they worked, checked everything they did, made capricious and arbitrary changes in the correspondence they wrote. Her response to any drop in productivity was to take hostages. Nobody went home until the work was done.

Some people who had only trivial dealings with Roberta mistook the self-satisfied expression on her face for pleasantness. Her employees knew better. She looked that way because she thought she was always right, smarter than anyone else.

When one of the clerks finally got up the nerve to quit, Roberta looked for a suitably passive replacement. Jim looked like just the guy. He was laid-back and easygoing, and best of all had been out of a job for several months. Roberta imagined that he was cowed enough by that experience to buckle down to her regimen of overwork and insults. Not this time. Jim never got upset, yet he never rebelled. He said yes to whatever Roberta asked and worked at his own pace. He rarely made mistakes, but he did only what he had to. When Roberta criticized him, he smiled knowingly, listened, but neither answered nor smarted under her snide remarks. Sometimes when she stood next to his desk to look at his work, he hauled his six-foot, four-inch frame out of the chair and sat on the desk and looked her right in the eye. He wasn't insubordinate. He just nodded and smiled. It drove Roberta crazy. But it inspired the rest of the department. They saw that Jim never got into trouble and never really knuckled under. They learned that if they didn't want to be bullied, they didn't have to be. Neither do you.

HOW BOSSES USE POWER

Bosses always have some power. The possession of that power is not in itself a problem. Power relationships can be good as well as bad. When you and your boss share goals and use your skills for mutual benefit, the power relationship is healthy. But when the boss overdoes the role of evaluator and guide and turns it into a power trip, you've got trouble.

You can spot the boss on a power trip by any of a number of behaviors. There is the "me first, last, and only" routine. These bosses become outraged when you try to make a decision. They prefer to have ventriloquists' dummies for subordinates. They prefer to solve all the problems. They must have all the bright ideas. They turn the modern office or plant into a sweatshop by hogging all the interesting work and giving you only the drudgery. They take all the credit; you take all the blame.

These malicious managers are harsh in their

criticisms. They emphasize mistakes, but overlook employees' achievements. They are insensitive to your human needs. They censure you when you are vulnerable, and criticize you in public. A favorite bully tactic is to criticize subordinate managers in front of their employees.

Yet these thugs want only good news themselves. They play kill the messenger. They resort to the worst form of corporate terrorism—they threaten to fire you.

Slave drivers, of course, pile on the work. They make exorbitant demands, set unreasonable deadlines. Ray Fisher's boss had a habit of calling him in at 4:30 and giving him rush assignments that had to be done before he went home. He kept Ray running constantly, not just with work at the plant but with personal chores like picking up the boss's kids at nursery school or taking the boss's car to be inspected. Ray never heard his boss say thank you. Yet Ray never stood up to his boss. He never took any steps to rectify his situation. Everyone in the office, even the computer service rep who came in once a month, knew that Ray was unhappy. Everyone, that is, except the boss.

This is often the way with tyrants. People keep things from them. If they sense this, they become suspicious. Petty dictators like to know everything. There is a difference between their morbid curiosity and the legitimate needs of a manager to know what's going on in the department. These bullies are looking for information so they can mug somebody with it later. They use not only threats of retaliation but promises of rewards to extort or manipulate more work out of people. If they can't break down resistance with threats and coercion, they use hard sell techniques. They just don't hear your objection or they use guilt to get you to comply—they say you're "not a team player."

Winnie Gallagher worked as an assistant buyer in a department store. Her boss, Mary Ann, daily showed her how little she thought of her. Mary Ann would call Winnie in for a meeting and then keep her waiting. Then, in the middle of their meeting, Mary Ann would answer phone calls. Winnie would find herself talking to the top of Mary Ann's head while Mary Ann read the mail during a discussion of a critical project.

At meetings with Mary Ann's boss, the moment Winnie started to talk, Mary Ann would suddenly start to pay more attention to her fingernails than to the facts Winnie was presenting. Winnie often left those meetings and went into the women's room to cry. She was humiliated, angry, and frustrated all at once. One day, at her sister's house, Winnie broke down completely. "Is it me? It must be me," she said. She vowed to get back at Mary Ann, to make her look bad in front of the sales people who came in to call. She said she'd quit. She decided to go to personnel and complain. She wondered whether Mary Ann was jealous of her, but couldn't figure out why she should be. She fantasized that Mary Ann would be fired. Finally, at her sister's urging, Winnie decided to confront Mary Ann about her disdainful behavior. She hoped to gain Mary Ann's respect and open a dialogue that would heal the rift between them.

What she got instead was a lecture on being overly sensitive. "You'll never get anywhere in this business with that thin skin of yours. Toughen up or take off," Mary Ann said as she rubbed some carpet fuzz off her shoe. Eventually Winnie left for another job. But when she finally quit, her stock of confidence was flat.

Tyrants rob you of self-respect. On the surface it may seem unimportant that some bosses insist on being called Mr. or Ms. while their kids call you by your first name. You may not see the boss's feet on the desk as a conscious power play. But these gestures are symbolic. They establish the boss's supremacy, confirm the sultan's superiority. Bosses who ask you a question and then start reading the mail while you answer are, consciously or unconsciously, communicating their disdain for your opinions. When they interrupt your work or your phone calls with their petty requests, when they move you arbitrarily from project to project, when they ask you to do personal errands on company time, they scorn, subtly or blatantly, your contribution to the important work of the organization.

EFFECTS OF
SLAVE DRIVING
MANAGEMENT

Unfortunately, these tyrannical bosses succeed, at least in the short run. At first, they get a lot of work out of people. Through intimidation, they do win their battles. In the long run the organization and the employees lose the war.

Sometimes such a manager can create an opposition group among his or her subordinates. The marketing group in one international organization had a terrible reputation as a place to work because of the nasty tactics of the marketing vice president. He created a turnover rate of over 60 percent. It was easy to see how. Management by stress was his credo. He delighted in giving new people impossible assignments, such as insisting that they choose among three promotions, each preposterous in terms of the product's marketing goals. Not bad, you might say, as a learning experience for a trainee. Yes, but . . . the exercise was set up in such a way that there was no right answer, but the vp insisted that the trainees pick one. When the trainees presented their conclusions at a department meeting, he humiliated them publicly, belittling their choices and attacking them personally.

When I met the people who worked there, they were extremely supportive of one another. They had banded together to defend themselves against their common enemy—the boss. The organization did reap some interim benefits from the teamwork created by the boss's abusive behavior. In the long run, though, such a cabal can turn into a junta intent on ousting the boss. They may spend more time trying to unseat the person in authority than working toward the organization's goals.

The high turnover created by slave drivers is

enough to make them long-term failures as managers. That and absenteeism. People just don't come to work every day if they have to face abuse and vilification. If your boss gives you a headache, you don't bother to go to work if you already have one. If a boss insists upon hearing only good news, the bad news doesn't go away. The bump under the rug grows until everyone starts to trip over it. Eventually, the people who really care about their own success leave organizations where the browbeaters are in charge. Productivity suffers.

Working for Attila takes its toll on you. Stress is the obvious problem, and it's a killer. If your boss is a worrywart, she may give herself an ulcer; if she's a slave driver, she'll give you one. Pressure for more and more output is one of the greatest causes of stress on the job. A lack of control over your own work is another. With corporate tyrants you get the double whammy. The result is physical illness.

Or the damage can be psychological. Through humiliation, the bully seeks to create a slave mentality among employees. If you make a mistake that embarrasses you, you need guidance and help to avoid the problem in the future. Instead this type of boss pours salt on your wounded ego. You and the people you work with will feel suspicious and insecure—definitely about the boss, and maybe even about each other.

Your motivation will suffer when your boss refuses to hear your ideas but only delights in giving you orders. If your boss gives you a chance to try out your own idea, you work hard to make the project succeed and prove yourself right. If your boss insists you do everything her way, your motivation (consciously or unconsciously) is to prove her wrong. In the one case, you both succeed. In the latter, you fail. And with this type of boss you fail alone.

If your boss's goals are incompatible with yours, you work against one another. Communication, the crux of a good boss-subordinate relationship, suffers. That's what happened between Barbara Berquist and her boss, Marty.

Marty was always rattling daggers. Barbara supervised a group of order-takers for a major plastic packaging manufacturer. Barbara's objective with her group was to have them process the same day every order that came in before 3:45 p.m. Marty agreed wholeheartedly with that goal. But Barbara felt that as long as her people accomplished their tasks, she wasn't going to rag them about taking a little extra time at a break or wearing blue jeans to the office. Not so Marty, the perfectionist. He felt he had made it to his manager's spot because of his devotion to detail. Nothing escaped him. He and Barbara clashed constantly about issues peripheral to the work, things Barbara considered minutiae that would only antagonize the staff and spoil their team spirit.

Marty insisted on strict enforcement of the "rules." At a performance review he repeated his usual threat. "Listen, Barbara," he said, "they've given you a chance to prove yourself as a supervisor. If you can't keep that crowd of yours under

control, I can always find someone else who will."
Barbara had always heard the threat before, but
hadn't taken it seriously. Now that Marty made it
part of a formal performance appraisal, Barbara felt
she had no choice but to comply. She had worked
hard to earn her promotion to supervisor; she
wasn't going to give it up that easily. She decided
that her only choice was to ingratiate herself to
Marty. She became a constant companion to the
rule book. Barbara felt she could not let on that
Marty was the source of the new rigidity. She
hoped her people would realize it themselves, but
she said nothing to them. They never caught on.
They figured Barbara was buttering Marty up for
a promotion or a raise.

Barbara felt deprived of her power as a person
and especially as a supervisor. She turned sour.
Before long, morale in her unit hit rock bottom.
When the group started to miss its 3:45 goal, she
and Marty quarreled openly. Barbara swore it was
Marty's rigidity that had spoiled the group's morale. Marty said that if Barbara had not been so
lax with her people to begin with, they would never
have felt entitled to special privileges. They both
wound up angry. Marty because he used pressure
tactics that backfired, Barbara because she knuckled under and felt like a coward.

Forcing yourself to bend to your boss's pressure tactics will make you frustrated and hostile.
It will stall your career. Without motivation and
without learning, where can your career go? If you
start saying "yes" when you can't deliver, you'll

get a reputation for being undependable. Good-bye next promotion.

On the other hand, working under adverse conditions can help you. Many successful people claim they learned humility from working for a tyrant. Egotism might have ruined their future, but working for an ego-bruiser cleansed them of any arrogance they might have had.

You can also learn from a crummy boss what *not* to do when you become a manager yourself. In fact, since the lessons are so painful, you may learn better from a bad situation than you would from a good one. The suffering may encourage you to identify your own strengths and weaknesses and focus on what you have to offer and what you need to improve your own character. And there are productive things you can do to improve your situation.

ANTI-TYRANT TACTICS

First, make sure your expectations are realistic. Your goal should be to make yourself feel better, to make your work-life less stressful, and to put your career on a positive track. Your goal is not to change the boss's personality. Most psychologists agree that bullies' behavior stems from basic feelings of insecurity. Deep-rooted behaviors like those are really out of your reach to change. So don't expect pat answers or easy solutions.

Most people put up with autocratic bosses for a while, but eventually get fed up and leave. Some people try standing up to bullies and get fired. Some, who feel they have no other options, stick around. They just inure themselves to the bully's tactics. A Chicago-based engineering firm was nearly ruined by one bully. The responses of the employees of that firm were varied and variously successful in dealing with the pain and suffering he caused.

Jerry Ryle was one of his victims. After just seven years with the firm, Jerry was one of its most important project managers. He felt secure with his job and his accomplishments. People called his designs brilliant, and he agreed. He especially liked the close contact and recognition he got from the president of the firm. Now he was managing the largest project in the firm's history.

When the firm announced it would merge with a New York engineering company, Jerry felt disoriented. He dreaded changes that might affect his work. Most of the time mergers meant staff cuts, reorganizations, having to work in a chaotic atmosphere for a while. Jerry hated the idea. All the gossiping and jockeying for position that followed the announcement annoyed him, especially when he got sucked into it himself. And he did almost every lunchtime.

But Jerry also saw the up side of working for a larger firm. *With greater resources, he thought, we can bid on even larger jobs. I'll get to do even more challenging projects than the one I have now.* Jerry decided to look at the positive side of things. Some of his colleagues were worried about losing their jobs, but he was sure that his skill and reputation made him immune to dismissal.

The cold lump in the pit of Jerry's stomach didn't form until he heard a rumor that the president was moving to the New York headquarters of the new parent company. The next morning Jerry woke up at four o'clock. Later he would tell his wife Carol that the dog's scratching and thumping woke him up, but as he lay there he thought about what would happen in Chicago if the president moved to New York. Maybe they'll put Dennis in charge of the office, he thought. No, Dennis had enough trouble managing his own team of engineers. Maybe me. They won't. I'm the youngest, least experienced project manager. He thought that if he were in charge he would give the drafting department more space. He pictured himself taking over the president's old office. In the end, he decided he wouldn't get the job and he really didn't want it. He got up to shave at five and was in the office by seven that morning. He didn't have to wait long to find out what everyone in the firm was burning to know.

The president was, indeed, leaving, and New York was sending out someone named Keith Morris to run Chicago. A few days later Keith arrived. The first thing Jerry noticed about him was his size. He had the body of a weightlifter. Soon Jerry and everyone else in the firm found out that Keith also had the morals of a warlord.

Just before the president left, he met with the entire staff. He reassured them for the fifth or sixth time that no one would be fired as a result of the merger. He formally introduced Keith and said that Chicago should not worry about interference from New York. He and the CEO of the parent company had agreed that Chicago was doing very well on its own. They were giving Keith a free hand to run his operation.

At first Keith didn't use that hand very freely. In the next few weeks, he reorganized a minor project and asked a lot of questions. He took each of the project engineers out to lunch and seemed quite friendly. At their lunch together, Jerry was a bit disturbed by some of Keith's personal remarks about the other people in the firm. But he dismissed the gossip as an innocent attempt at camaraderie. That night Jerry told Carol that he thought Keith was okay. For a few days, Jerry slept until the alarm clock woke him up.

Exactly four weeks after Keith took over the office, he fired three engineers, a draftsman, and two computer operators. At lunch that day, Jerry and his friend Dennis, another project manager, talked about what Dennis called the pogrom. "Come on, Dennis," Jerry said, "he's just doing the new-broom-sweeps-clean routine. I read an article once that advised people who were taking over a company to fire someone to establish their authority. Besides, at least two of those people were dead weight to the organization. I've heard you say that yourself."

Over the next few weeks, as Keith's true personality emerged, Jerry thought back to how he had defended Keith at that lunch. *How could I have been so naive? he wondered.*

Almost every night Jerry came home with another horror story for Carol.

One night he was particularly disturbed. "I went to Keith today to talk to him about what he's doing to Maddy Hall," he said. Carol knew Maddy, the administrative supervisor for the firm. "He started dumping a lot of junk work on her. He asked her to reorganize the files just when she was strapped trying to get out the proposal for a plant expansion at Superior Foods. She told me she tried to talk over the problem with him, but he ignores her requests for a meeting. He belittles her. Anyway, I went to him to try to tell him how valuable she is to the firm, how everything the clients see that we do has to pass through her hands. You know what he said? He told me to mind my own business, that I had no authority in the administrative area." Carol thought Maddy should just leave the firm. Eventually Maddy did. Once again, the dog started to wake Jerry up before dawn every morning.

After work one evening, Jerry and Dennis speculated on what they would do. Dennis said, "I decided to protect myself. I've always been on good terms with Marshall North in the Houston office. I'm going to cement that relationship. He's the second most powerful person in the firm. He'll probably be the next president. He may not be able to stop Keith from badgering me on a day-to-day basis, but he can save my job if it's on the line."

173

"Maybe we should call the president in New York?" Jerry suggested. His voice was getting strained. Every time this damn subject came up, he could feel his throat tighten. And the subject came up every day.

"Forget it," Dennis said. "He's in Germany negotiating to buy out a firm there. Besides, Marshall says Keith is in with the CEO in New York. We'll never get rid of him."

Jerry felt Dennis was fairly safe from dismissal, at least for the time being. "And you're golden," Dennis told him. "You're the best engineer in the firm and everyone knows it." They speculated on who would be Keith's next victim. Jerry said he thought it might be Fran, the only woman project manager in the firm. "She stands up to him. He doesn't like that." Dennis disagreed. "He's too smart to risk a discrimination charge. Besides, Fran is running two projects for Universal Printing and Packaging and they love her over there. He's not about to mess up our relationship with them by making her unhappy. I think it's going to be Ross or somebody in accounting."

It turned out to be Jerry.

Jerry was disgusted with himself for watching morale slide and doing nothing about it. His people were beginning to show the strain of living with Keith's unpredictable temper. Besides, everyone in the firm was rumor-mongering instead of working. Jerry thought if he presented the morale problem in financial terms Keith would have to listen.

Keith listened. And then he blew up. Jerry told the story only to Carol and Dennis and his wife. At dinner over the weekend he said, "He called me arrogant and independent. He told me it was time to put me in my place."

Dennis stared into his beer. "I hate to tell you this Jerry, but maybe you'd better back off. He's been bad-mouthing you at the district manager's meeting. Marshall told me about it a couple of days ago. I wasn't going to say anything to you, but I'm afraid if you don't watch your step . . ."

Jerry was livid. He clenched his fist. "That SOB better not mess with me," he said. "I won't get mad; I'll get even." Carol prevailed upon Jerry to calm down. Dennis assured him that nothing Keith said could spoil his reputation for technical genius. "Besides, Jerry," he said, "this firm needs you more than you need it and he knows it."

A few days later, Keith transferred Jerry's secretary to a new job without consulting Jerry or the secretary. Take it or leave it was his attitude. Jerry's left eyeball started to hurt. He was rehearsing the argument in his head as he approached Keith's office. Without really intending to, he slammed the door. "What right have you got to make a decision like that without consulting me." Jerry realized he was shouting. His voice nearly broke. "This firm needs me more than I need it," he said as calmly as he could. "Either you treat me like the professional I am, or I'll quit."

When Keith smiled, Jerry saw that he was playing right into Keith's hands. He promised himself he would hold his temper. Get even; just get even, he told himself. He got up and left. Neither he nor Keith said another word.

Things were calm for the next week. Everyone figured Jerry had stood up to Keith and that it had worked. Jerry knew better, but he let them think he had been a man about the issue.

The peace was only temporary. And when war broke out again, it was worse than ever. Keith preempted some of Jerry's computer time for a new business proposal. When Jerry confronted him, saying he had caused the firm to miss an important deadline, Keith just got up and left the room. Jerry lost his cool completely. Afterward, he remembered thinking that he was about to do a stupid thing. But he followed Keith down the hall, still upset, still reminding him of the importance of the project he had interrupted. Keith turned around and grabbed Jerry by the lapels and shoved him against the wall. Jerry's body went cold. He stopped thinking or acting. With his nose a few inches from Jerry's face, Keith shouted criticism of Jerry at the top of his lungs.

Jerry didn't speak. He looked at the enlarged pores on Keith's face. He noticed that Keith's collar was too small. When Keith let him go and walked away, Jerry just went into his office and closed the door. He sat down and picked up a pencil and started to draw. Somewhere in his head he knew he should be thinking about what just happened to him and he was wondering why he wasn't thinking about it when Dennis came in.

"I heard what happened, Jerry. Are you all right? What a bastard. Does he think he can beat everyone into submission? You'd be within your rights to report him to the police."

Jerry didn't feel like talking to Dennis. "I'm all right, Den," he said. "I shouldn't have followed him down the hall. I appreciate your concern, but right now I think I want to call Carol and talk to her for a few minutes."

After Dennis left, Jerry called his wife at her office. "Carol, something has come up here. I need to talk to you. Can you meet me for lunch?"

Jerry couldn't wait for lunch. He left the office right away and walked around. His head was swimming with ideas. It occurred to him that he should be angry and feel vindictive, but for some reason he didn't. All he could think about was how free he felt. When he met Carol at the restaurant, he didn't even tell her, at least not at the beginning, what had happened to him. He just said, "How would you feel about my starting my own business?"

By the time their sandwiches arrived, Jerry was telling Carol how he would market his services as free-lance design engineer. He was afraid that Carol's first supportive reaction might disappear by nightfall, but he felt he had to go ahead. His own resolve wavered sometimes in his mind, but he didn't let on to Carol that he had doubts. He wondered if she knew he was convincing himself as well as her when he said, "I know there are big risks in this, but we've talked about it on and off as something I would do someday. If I'm ever going to start my own thing, I better do it now while I have the energy and the time to recuperate if it doesn't work out. Besides, I just can't stand to work for that bastard another day." Then, he told Carol how Keith had assaulted him.

They decided Jerry would have to stay on the job a while longer, at least until he had a commitment from one client. He went back to the office, flipped through his Rolodex, and wrote down the phone numbers of twelve key people. He woke up early again the next morning and at first he lay in bed thinking about how Keith had humiliated him. But finally, he just got up and started making lists and plans. That day he called six of the people on his list and made appointments. His friends at the office asked him leading questions, but he was careful not to let anyone know what he was doing. Not even Dennis.

Jerry was hardly ever around at lunchtime to find out if Dennis suspected anything. He was too busy trying to line up clients. He got a cool reception from the first few people. They told him how much they appreciated the good work he had done in the past, but they worried about entrusting a project to a brand new free-lancer. He was about two-thirds of the way through his list when he finally got the response he wanted.

"What took you so long?" was the reaction of Rich Simonetti of National Department Stores. "I figured as soon as the merger took place, you'd see the handwriting on the wall and do your own thing."

Jerry was tempted to tell Rich about the problems he'd been having with Keith, but he held his tongue. He stuck to getting information about up-

coming projects and ended by agreeing to send
Rich a proposal on a new clothing warehouse in
Gary, Indiana. "I can't promise you anything," Rich
said. "You know that these decisions are always
made by committees, but I'll do my best to get
you the job."

"That's enough for me, Rich," Jerry said, when
he really would have preferred a guarantee. He
knew he would have to wait. He did. In the
meantime, he kept his head low at the office and
threw Dennis off the trail by occasionally discussing byzantine political strategies for Keith's undo-
ing. He called on a couple of other potential clients
who said they would consider him for future work.
The most promising, Helmut Meat Packing, said
that as soon as he was established on his own,
they would give him a project. But he got no contracts and no word came from Rich Simonetti.
Weeks went by.

He and Carol were starting to talk more often
about his just getting a job with another engineering firm when Rich called. He wanted some
changes in the proposal, but it was definitely alive
and well.

National never got such a fast revision. Jerry
and Carol were up till two-fifteen in the morning
printing it on their home computer. A messenger
delivered it the next day.

Still three weeks went by before Rich responded. Jerry was out of town on a job when it
came. Carol called him at the Holiday Inn in Kan-
kakee to tell him. He had the National contract.

When he told his friends in the office that he

was leaving, Jerry felt a small twinge of guilt. He felt triumphant about his contract and hopeful about his future. He knew most of them were happy for him. But quite a few did say he was walking away with one of their best clients. He never said a word to Keith. A year later, when his old company was on the brink of ruin, Dennis told Jerry that Keith had been fired. It took two years for the firm to recover its former position. Jerry listened to Dennis's gossip about what was going on in the firm and was gratified when Keith finally got his comeuppance. Most of the time, though, Jerry was too involved in his own business to think much about it.

HERE'S WHAT YOU CAN DO

Combating tactics like Keith's is a delicate and ultimately frustrating undertaking. But if you are faced with a slave driver or a bully for a boss, you must protect your health and motivation. Jerry decided to be his own boss. That's a possibility. Profiles of successful entrepreneurs show that among many other qualities, most of them have had a bad experience working for someone else. A boss like Keith could be just the catalyst you need to make you determined to succeed on your own.

But not everyone can do as Jerry did and start a business. Some of us are neither financially nor psychologically prepared to take such a risk. Working for someone may be your only choice.

But that doesn't mean you have to take whatever is handed to you. Here are some steps you can take to fight back.

First, stop being a victim. You are in charge of your own attitude. You decide to be a winner or a loser. Choose winning. Remember, bullies pick their victims. If you stop acting like a victim, your bully boss will have to go elsewhere for the satisfaction of his or her superiority needs. Jerry's friend Dennis chose to protect himself by playing the political game. He got himself a powerful ally to shield him from Keith's temper. If this sort of safeguard will give you the confidence you need, fine. The strength to hold your own against the Keiths of this world may come from inside you or from outside circumstances you arrange for yourself, just as long as you find that strength. And remember, if you refuse to be coerced, you won't be. If you stand your ground calmly and do your job without losing your temper or succumbing to the undue pressure, you can win. In the end, it's the hammer, not the anvil, that breaks.

Like Maddy Hall, the administrative supervisor whom Jerry tried to defend, you may find it easier just to leave your dictator boss behind and find another job. If other jobs are available, that's an option. But you may be reluctant to leave the company before your pension is vested. Or you may like the company and your colleagues so much that you decide to wait it out and see if you get a new boss soon. Or you may decide that your boss is a tyrant but, unlike Keith, has other redeeming qualities—such as superior knowledge or skill—that make you want to stick around.

IF YOU DECIDE TO STAY

Make the most of your relationship with your boss. Concentrate on mutual gains. If your boss isn't completely hideous, concentrate on your common aims, and stop working at cross-purposes.

Approach the slave driver gingerly. Make sure your tone is friendly and any complaints are matter-of-fact. Simple, straightforward discussions about what needs to be done in the future may be productive. Long accusations about her past transgressions will certainly end in new power plays. Amateur psychoanalysis is out for both of you.

Ask questions; don't issue ultimatums. Challenge the course of action or the decision, but not the boss's authority. Once the discussion is over, summarize it in writing; document any agreements you've reached. Give a copy of the summary to the boss; keep one in your CYA file.

Make sure your behavior is consistent. If you succumb to threats even part of the time, they will not go away.

Learn to counter tyrannical tactics. For instance, if your boss is nosy, be generous with information you want to share. Tell him about potential problems before you are asked. That way you will seem open and honest. If you seem to be hiding something, your boss will get even more suspicious and prying.

Avoid triggering the boss's temper. If your boss wants only good news, find a neutral way to communicate the bad news. Reports that are generated automatically will be best, especially if they seem to come from a large group or, better yet, a computer.

Don't lose your temper. Insults from the boss can be hardest to take. No matter how personal they seem, try to remember that you are probably just a convenient victim, that the boss is looking for somewhere to vent his spleen, and that you just happened by. Power players delight in getting other people's goats. Hang on to your goat for dear life. Use a matter-of-fact tone and express your own point of view with as much cool as you can muster. Suppose your boss says, "This quarterly analysis is totally incoherent. You are so stupid, I'm surprised you can find your car in the parking lot three days out of five." Your immediate response is to lash back with an equally stinging remark. But remember, your boss only talks that way to rile you. Instead say, "I'm certain the figures in the report are correct. Which of the conclusions do you take issue with?" It will be very hard to keep your temper this way, but it will be worth the effort. Your boss will not have succeeded in upsetting you. People don't keep dropping bombs if the bombs don't explode.

Don't stand for rude behavior. If your boss stops paying attention when you are in the middle of saying something, offer to come back at a more convenient time. But don't go away without making a specific date. Then, when the day comes, you can remind him that the time was set aside for your discussion. Apply some pressure to get the attention you deserve.

When the boss approaches your desk with more work, stand up and talk about it. If she starts to discuss your shortcomings in public, offer to step into an office or a conference room before you continue the discussion. If you are sitting or, worse, standing in front of the boss's desk while you're being chastised, pull a chair around and sit on the same side of the desk with him.

Make your efforts obvious. With a slave driver, if you make the job look easy, you may convince the boss that you just aren't trying. Some people use humor. You see signs all over offices and plants that say things like, "We the unwilling, led by the unfeeling, have attempted the improbable so often and for so long, that we now accept the impossible as a matter of policy." One foreman said to his boss, who had just given him the fifth special project of that month, "Great, Jack, I'm glad to take this on. Having so many new things to learn in one month has convinced me that you are grooming me for a big promotion very soon. Margaret and I were talking this over at dinner last night. We are just trying to figure out whether to buy a new car or take a trip with the big raise that must be coming."

Be prepared to oppose the sales pitch. Dictators don't brook any resistance to their ideas. If you object and your boss immediately resorts to the hard sell to sway you, don't just cave in. Without insisting, press for the decision you want. If you're afraid the boss will ignore your counter arguments, listen to what she has to say and ask for some time to think it over. Put your analysis in a memo, offering your own solution to the problem. Some bosses who cannot stand to be challenged in person will read a report written in an objective tone.

Pick your fights. Don't try to win every point. There will be issues that are trivial to you but important to the boss. Give in on those.

Learn to recognize the tacky tactics. If your boss is tricky, he may claim that "top management" is putting on the pressure. He may appeal to your "team spirit," threaten reprisals, or make empty promises of great rewards. There are a million of these. Once you know which ones your boss is likely to use, you can spot them coming. Then, just name them out loud. "Benny, if I didn't know you I might think you were bringing these complaints up at 4:30 just to make sure I wouldn't have time to respond properly. I'm sure that's not the case, so why don't we just wait until the morning and discuss them." Once a person is caught trying a shabby trick, it loses its potency.

Don't be overly intimidated by threats of being fired. You've probably read that employers' rights to "termination at will" are being challenged in court. And companies are losing cases. Besides, in larger companies, most managers do not have the sole authority to fire employees. You may find that your boss has less power in this regard than you think. This may give you the confidence you need to show your spunk and try to rectify your problems with the boss.

Sometimes none of these suggestions works. Your boss may be so callous or irrational that you will run out of patience and decide to get another job. While you are looking for one, develop your patience and use passive resistance to avoid complete slavery. Be placid, but do only what you can with a reasonable amount of effort. Clam up completely when the boss is on the rampage. While you are looking for a better job, understand that you are staying *temporarily* because being there serves your needs. If you remind yourself that you are there by choice, you'll stop feeling like a dupe.

8

VACILLATORS, WEAKLINGS, AND PHANTOMS

*I was a-trembling because
I'd got to decide.*

Mark Twain
*Adventures of
Huckleberry Finn*

We feel like we're on the deck of a ship and no one's at the helm," they told me. I had been called in to solve a morale problem at a small subsidiary of a larger client company. The cause of the employee dissatisfaction soon became clear. The people in the organization were not suffering from harsh management. It was not that their managers had tried managing and failed. It was that they weren't managing at all. The president was distracted by his dealings with the parent company. Without any leadership from above, the next level of managers was in disarray. Some were too concerned with their own careers to pay much attention to their people. Others were floundering, trying to guess what was needed or wanted. Middle managers switched direction constantly. Employees said priorities changed so often that if you drew up a list you had to put not only the date, but also the time on the piece of paper.

Muddled managers come in three varieties: those who haven't got the guts to give clear direction—the Weaklings; those who change the rules constantly—the Vacillators; and those who are just not around to guide and encourage their people— the Phantoms. I put them together here because they seem to have common causes, produce similar results, and require like responses.

Good managers communicate an extraordinary focus on goals. This attracts similar commitment from their employees. Without this dedication to the work, managers appear weak. The troops are always loath to follow a leader who doesn't seem to know where he's going.

HOW BOSSES
LOSE THEIR WAY

Some bosses are so busy doing "their own work" that they have no time to manage. In their book *In Search of Excellence*, Tom Peters and Robert Waterman made a great deal of the technique they called MBWA (Management By Walking Around). Business people all over the United States greeted this as a revolutionary and inspired notion. Managers should stay in contact with the people who work for them. What a great new concept! It tells you what a sorry pass management has come to that managers have to be reminded of something as basic as talking to and listening to their employees.

Some managers get out of touch because they burn out. The workaholics put in so much, strive so furiously. After a while, they begin to plod through their daily work activities practically insensate. Some become ill from the stress. A boss who is in the hospital certainly can't manage. Neither can one who still comes to work but whose eyes are permanently glazed over.

Stanley Graham simply lost faith in the organization and its goals. He works for an international chemical company. He wasn't setting any records as a manager and he knew his annual salary would never equal his army serial number, but he was doing his job and doing it well. Then a major catastrophe happened. Suddenly, the company name was in the headlines and the organization looked bad. After nearly fifteen years with the company, Stan was ashamed to tell people where he worked. Neighbors and friends who already knew asked him embarrassing questions; they made accusations against the company, and Stan had no defense. Suddenly going to work really depressed him. This once decent manager just isn't turned on to the work anymore. He used to do his job well; now he's just going through the motions.

WEAKLINGS

Like Stan, some bosses lose their devotion to the job. Other bosses never even take up the managerial "reigns" in the first place. They accept the management job when someone offers it because they want the prestige or the money or the perks, but they are uncomfortable with the power and insecure about themselves as managers. They are indecisive and confused. They are afraid to ask their employees to do anything. Sometimes they supervise people who were their colleagues and friends, and they fear alienating or offending them. They don't know how to take charge without being bossy so they don't take charge at all. They keep a low profile and hope that the years to retirement will pass quickly.

Your weak boss may avoid managing important issues by staying enmeshed in trivia. This managerial mistake can go two ways. Like Captain Queeg with the strawberries and the shirttails, the boss can dramatize trivia while the organization goes around in circles. Perhaps, instead, your boss makes molehills out of mountains, overlooks critical issues, or misses important opportunities. In any case, the boss will look like a fool or a villain to you.

Secretaries often see the worst sort of weakling boss behavior. Managers expect their secretaries to mother them, get them food and things to drink, tidy up after them, and chase them around if their stockbrokers call. Norma DiCarlo's boss was one such dependent. Then, perhaps because of his general weakness as a manager, he was removed from his job. Everybody in the department rejoiced, certain that they would get some decent leadership at last. Norma also hoped the new boss would be an improvement, but she hardly got a chance to find out. Her old boss called her constantly, asking for favors, complaining about his new assignment, looking for someone to soothe his bruised ego. His calls took up her time and distracted her from her work. After years of reporting to him, she found it difficult to put him off and refuse his pleas. She didn't get rid of his interruptions until he retired seventeen months later.

CHANGEABLE BOSSES

Like weaklings, vacillators are also uncomfortable with power. They try to do their jobs, but they haven't got the guts to stick to their guns. They make a decision but become so fearful that it may backfire that they unmake it and make another one. They spend so much time trying to see all sides of the issue that they never make up their minds. They transmit indecision or less urgency than the situation merits.

Their insecurity also causes them to vacillate in their management style. Muriel Solomon worked in an insurance company as a cost analyst. She was good at her job and got along well with the other people in her group. She was, frankly, a little surprised when they made her manager of cost analysis. One of her main worries was that the people who used to be her friends wouldn't like her anymore. So when she first took over as manager she tried to be very low-key. She knew the other analysts knew their jobs and liked her, and she hoped that would be enough. She left them pretty much alone.

Soon she noticed a drop in productivity. "They're goofing off," she thought. She decided to watch for signs of time-wasting and nip them in the bud. When she saw people talking to one another, she scolded them for socializing. Soon the whole place was buzzing with the news that Muriel had turned into a tyrant, that her promotion had gone to her head.

Next Muriel noticed that people were avoiding

her, looking very busy when she came by. "I've overdone it," she thought. "They think I'm a shrew." So she tried to make people understand that she still wanted to be friends. She asked about their families and their social activities, and went around the department chatting everyone up. But then, when she saw them talking among themselves a great deal, she decided they were taking advantage of her friendliness and turned cold and scolding again.

From her employees' perspective Muriel looked like a schizo, leaping from one set of behaviors to another for no particular reason. Soon they began to ask the secretary, "What kind of mood is she in today?" before they approached her.

A few vacillating bosses are indeed mentally ill, some temporarily because they are dealing with serious personal problems, others permanently because they have suffered whatever damage causes people to go off their rockers. Some are highly neurotic and difficult to deal with; a handful are so seriously bent that they need medical attention. Remember, since we've ruled out amateur psychoanalysis, your purpose is to learn how to deal with these people, not how to cure them.

Management training (my life's work for the past twenty-two years) can induce vacillation in management style. Bad management trainers, explicitly or implicitly, seek to change the personalities of the managers they instruct. They ignore the fact that personality transformations are impossible to accomplish in a few days, especially with unwilling adult subjects. They tell participants that to become better managers they must adopt certain traits and characteristics. Often they are very persuasive in their appeals for more understanding and kindness toward employees.

Managers can return from training sessions determined to make themselves into warm, fuzzy people that everyone will love and admire and try to emulate. The problem is that if these new characteristics are not natural to the managers' personalities, they can't keep up this facade for long. They revert to their basic natures and act as they have in the past. Later, they may feel guilty about their backsliding and rededicate themselves to the new management religion they learned in the training session. This pendulum could swing for a while before things settle down. The rash of popular management books has led to what *BusinessWeek* magazine called "management by bestseller," where managers try out the latest fad and change their styles of management the way fashion models change their hairstyles—to fit the mode of the moment.

IT'S TEN A.M.; DO YOU KNOW WHERE YOUR BOSS IS?

Your boss may be neither a weakling nor a vacillator. Perhaps your boss is simply never around. In this case, it's not that you can't get clear direction, it's that you can't get any direction.

For some bosses, being away is a legitimate business necessity. They may be located in another building or city or state. Or they may need to be on the road often. If you work for "an empty chair," you need to take some special steps to work out a satisfying manager-employee relationship. And you must make sure you keep the boss informed. Many mindless decisions are made by bosses who don't have day-to-day contact with the work. You need to set up systems to avoid trouble.

Some bosses are in the office, but they are unnecessarily preoccupied with other matters. What kept Jemil Kasim's boss busy was impressing his boss. Jemil worked as a customer service manager for a long distance phone company. Her boss, Andre Canastel, was too busy currying favor with upper management to pay much attention to Jemil and her work.

When she tried to tell Andre about a rash of customer complaints connected with a new billing system, he told her he was too busy with "critical corporate matters" to get involved. "You're a big girl, Jemil," he told her. "You have to learn to handle things."

Although the company required annual appraisals, Andre conveniently forgot to do Jemil's. When she reminded him, he made dates to do it but canceled them repeatedly. "I feel invisible," Jemil told me. "I have a boss with two backs and no front. At least if he has a front it never seems to be facing in my direction." Transferring to another job seemed the only answer for Jemil. If your boss ignores your existence, get out while you still have your self-confidence.

Or perhaps your phantom boss's self-confidence is the problem. Keeping out of the way may be his strategy for avoiding decisions and the concomitant risks. He won't have to deal with your complaints, your requests, or your problems if he isn't around to hear about them.

To me the saddest form of this avoidance of responsibility is drinking or taking drugs. Bosses who do are there, but they are not there. They are physically present, but they are anesthetized.

There are a few other ways your boss can dodge her duties or shirk her responsibilities. She can pretend not to understand the issue. She can stop your suggestion with the flash freeze: "That's against company policy." She can just refuse to deal with the problem. Under the rug has long been a favorite hiding place for dirt.

Some ostrich bosses avoid difficulties by making it known that they don't want to hear anything negative. If you've been punished for bringing up bad news, you learn to hide it from the boss. He doesn't have to suppress the information; you do it for him.

There are some sly and tacky tactics in the game of avoiding decision making. If you often hear any of the following, you should be suspicious that the boss is a dodger: "I need more data." "It's not our problem; we didn't create this situation; they did. Let them solve it." "Why did you let this happen in the first place?" "I haven't got the authority to approve this." "What will the president (or the department head or the personnel department) think?" "That's a good idea, but . . ." (fill in the blank with a series of convenient objections). "Let's bring in someone who has some real expertise before we decide." Or the easiest delaying tactic in the history of bureaucratic chickenstuff: "Write me a memo on that."

I had a boss who believed in the adage "when the going gets tough, the tough get going." Whenever a decision had to be made, he left.

EFFECTS OF
NON-MANAGEMENT

Powerless or directionless bosses hurt the organizations they work for. Their failure to guide their people undermines the organization's ability to meet its goals. With turned-off management, employees wind up saying, "If she doesn't care, why should I?"

Without leadership, a company cannot be innovative. People in the ranks may be able to follow along with the rest of the industry, but lacking managerial support, regardless of how self-motivated the staff is, they can seldom do more than replicate what they have done in the past or imitate what others are doing.

A weak or vacillating boss can destroy your motivation and stunt your growth. Your coward boss won't let you try new methods because he's afraid you'll make mistakes. We say we learn by trial and error. If that's true, no mistakes means no learning. Your job will be ho-hum and your motivation will start taking days off even when you decide to drag yourself to work. Your career will make snail's progress.

Weak managers will also stunt your income growth. If your boss doesn't know how to use power and refuses to take risks, who will fight for good raises and promotions for you? In fact, weak bosses have trouble even getting you the resources you need to do your job well. The smallest budgets, the oldest equipment, and the meagerest staff levels are always found in the wimpiest boss's department.

Some outwardly macho bosses are really pantywaists underneath. Skip Boland had such a boss in Claude Racine. They worked for a software subsidiary of a large computer company. Skip considered Claude a good guy. In fact, when he transferred into Claude's group, one of his reasons for taking the job was the supportive approach Claude took in the interviews. Skip decided that moving his home and family was worth it since he would have an opportunity to try out new ideas in his new job, and he was confident that his creativity would put him on the fast track. His first assignment was an easy one, but he expected that. Claude wouldn't put him on something super tough right off the bat. Skip expected to have to prove himself before being assigned to work with the major clients.

Skip is patient, as most people in his business are. It took a while for the letdown to hit him. But eventually he began to chafe under a series of what he considered go-nowhere assignments. He began to worry about his progress, professionally and financially. When raise time came along, Skip was disappointed, but not shocked that he didn't get what he expected. He did, however, express his disappointment to Claude. Claude talked about how he went to bat for Skip at compensation meetings. Claude said, "We don't always win those battles at first, but at least they know what I want for you." Claude expected the pressure he was putting on to pay back at some point. At least that's what he told Skip.

Skip decided to review his job with Claude. He asked for a meeting and told Claude he wanted to discuss his assignments and how they related to his raises and his future. At first, Claude put him off with a bunch of excuses about deadlines and important management meetings. It took all Skip's perseverence just to get Claude to sit down and talk. *Where is that nice, open person who interviewed me for this job? Skip wondered.*

The results of that meeting (when it finally did occur) weren't perfect in Skip's mind, but Claude did agree to give him more challenging assignments. He even kept his word. Almost immediately, he gave Skip an assignment he could really bite into. The only disappointment was that he wanted to go with Skip to make the proposal to the client. Skip didn't like having the boss looking over his shoulder. But he went to work on the assignment, happy for a challenge at last.

In a few weeks, Skip had worked up some ideas he was very proud of. The project wasn't for a major client, but the ideas could have wider application. Skip was happy with his work for the first time since joining the department. Knowing Claude wasn't the rugged risk taker he pretended to be, Skip decided to present his design to Claude and get approval before the client presentation. When he asked his wife Maggie to listen while he practiced his presentation to Claude, Maggie was puzzled.

"Why are you presenting this to Claude," she asked. "Don't you usually bring your presentations right to the client?"

"He's still acting a little strange," Skip said. "He's coming to the client meeting. He seems skittish. I'm not sure how he'll react when the chips are down, so I figure I better get him to sign off on this idea before I present it to the client. The idea isn't really radical, but it is a little unusual; Claude may need to get used to it."

The next day, Claude listened to Skip's idea. Skip decided to give him the hard sell. He explained his approach and told Claude how anxious he was to get the clients to buy it. "I'm sure," Skip said, "this will wow them, and we'll be able to use their experience to sell the same idea to other companies."

Claude took the bait. "Go get 'em" was his cry. Skip figured he had finally gotten the break he needed. Not even Claude's cold feet would stand in his way once he scored big with a couple of major clients. He took Maggie out for a good dinner the night before the big client presentation.

Dressed in his best impress-the-client suit, Skip arrived early at the client's office and found Claude waiting for him in the reception room. "Boy," he thought, "I imagined I was ahead of schedule, but the boss got here before me."

When the time came for the meeting, it surprised Skip that Claude did not take the seat next to him at the conference table. Instead, after Skip sat down, Claude continued to make small talk with the vice president of operations of the client company. As the meeting was about to start Claude sat down next to the VP. Later Skip thought, "I should have seen the signs."

But at the time Skip was too excited and nervous to react to Claude's odd behavior. He waited for Claude to say a few words, and he stood up to give his presentation.

Everything went well until the question and answer period. All of a sudden, the data processing manager of the client company attacked Skip. He asked questions designed to embarrass him, to trip him up, to disprove his assumptions. Skip tried to keep his cool; in fact, he did keep his cool. He never blew off any steam until he got home. Claude's behavior was another matter.

As soon as the data processing manager started his attack, Skip began to look to Claude for moral support. None came. Instead, Claude remained what he later called "objective." Skip never thought of it as anything but chickenhearted.

In the discussion that followed, the operations vice president seemed to beg Claude to say something positive, to give a rationale that would counter the D.P. guy's mostly irrational objections. No such luck for Skip or the project. In fact, when pressed for an opinion, Claude suggested that they all needed more time to think. "Perhaps," he said, "Skip needs to reconsider his design and come up with something we can all be sure is reliable." In the end, Skip's design went down the tubes, and so did his motivation.

His biggest slide came right after that meeting. Claude insisted he come up with a conventional design. He gave up his elegant solution; he did his duty. "They say they want new ideas," he told his brother Andy, "but they want old new, not new new. So I give them old new. I save my energy for my golf game. Now, there's a game worth some effort."

Four years later, Claude took early retirement. The new group head looked at Skip's file and concluded that Skip's motivation might be revived with some encouragement. Even though Skip looked like just another piece of deadwood, the new boss tempted him to fan the embers of his motivation and see if he could find a spark. One of his techniques was to tease Skip privately by calling him one of Claude's boys. This infuriated Skip. Eventually, it was that fury that ignited Skip's spirit.

In eighteen months, Skip was functioning at his old level. He did a great deal of soul-searching and learned some of what he had done wrong in handling his situation with Claude. He never forgave Claude for being such a wimp, but he did start to move up in his job and feel good about it. He wound up about five years behind where he had hoped to be, but he felt he was a steadier person than he would have been if he had never had to deal with Claude. When his dedication to the job returned, his golf game suffered a little, but he didn't seem to mind.

Skip's new group head was a splendid manager. And Skip was lucky that someone came along eventually to revive his pride in himself. Otherwise, he would have become a permanent member of the petrified forest.

You may rationalize the death of your own ambition by blaming your boss. But you will be the loser. Things usually go the way they did with Skip and Claude. Claude retired in what looked remarkably like contentment, and Skip's frustration nearly killed his career.

COPING WITH WEAKLINGS, VACILLATORS, AND PHANTOMS

First, recognize and deal with your own self-doubts. If you don't know what you're afraid of, what you avoid confronting and why, you'll never know whether it's the boss's fears or your own that are causing the problems. Besides, how can you begin to combat the boss's fears if you don't understand your own?

Learn to boost the boss's confidence in you and your work by researching and backing up your ideas with data. Reassure the boss so he'll have the guts to stand by your recommendations.

In dealing with the vacillator, write things down. When you and the boss agree on something, put it in writing. This may seem like one of the more odious bureaucratic habits, but at least you will have a line of defense when the boss later "forgets" what she said. Also, some minor league vacillators may be deterred from making changes if they see those agreements written in official looking documents. You never know.

Learn to predict the boss's moods and time your moves. If you have a tough sell on your hands, ask for approval when you have something happy to report. People who work for drunks will approach the boss only in the morning or only in the afternoon, depending on the boss's reaction to the booze.

I once had a boss who never liked to give an unqualified yes. So I always approached him with several requests at once, and I always planted a throwaway suggestion on my list—something that sounded plausible but that I didn't really care about. Over time, I learned I could unerringly predict which request he would deny. I got him to agree with everything I really wanted. I don't think he ever suspected.

If your boss is an ostrich, don't try to make the bird face every problem. Be content if you can get her to deal with major issues and important changes. Beware the boss who tries to shift the burden of decision-making on to you. In some cases these "super-delegators" are good for your development. You grow and learn because they push off decisions and difficult work on you. Go ahead and grab the increased responsibility with both hands, provided you have a safety hatch if your decisions go sour. In theory, upper management should hold the boss responsible for screw-ups, especially if he abdicated his responsibility. Whenever someone says "in theory" you know that things don't usually work out that way in practice. Because your boss has greater access to upper management, he may dump the problem on you and then stick you with the rap for the botched decision.

Make the most of your time with the phantom. Keep a list of questions for the boss, and nab her when she is there. Get as much information as you can. Knowing what's going on is critical when you have to work independently and make judgments on your own. It's fair to remind your absentee boss of this quite directly. Paraphrase this paragraph as a preamble to your request for better communication.

Conversely, you need to set up a system for giving information to your phantom manager. Write regular reports or record notes on a tape to keep the boss informed of what you're doing. If your boss is a coward and is away a lot, schedule brief meetings to plan how you should handle decisions that must be made while he is away. A regular meeting works best for this, if you can get him to commit to such a thing. You may also want to document decisions you make in his absence and the rationale behind your choice.

A boss who won't be around for an important meeting can often smooth the way for you or get you the cooperation you need by making a phone call and letting people know that you represent him. Such "status transfer" doesn't always work, but it's worth a try. If you are going to take your absentee boss's place at a meeting, anticipate that you might have trouble with someone who balks at working with a "lower level" person. Ask your boss to call or write requesting the others at the meeting to give you their support.

Unlike slave drivers and bullies, weaklings, vacillators, and phantoms are often bearable if we learn to work around them. If you don't get knots in your stomach from thinking about how you do the work and he gets the pay and status, then maybe you can hang in. It may be worth it to you for the training, for the experience, or in the hopes that you will eventually get his job. If you decided on this route, just work for the best possible results and try to see your effectiveness as its own reward.

If your boss's inability to make a decision sends your blood pressure into orbit, then go find yourself a more reliable leader.

9

CHEAPSKATES

*. . . for the laborer
deserves his wages.*

Luke 10:8

As far as I can see,
money is a more taboo subject than sex. If you
don't believe me, think about this: you have friends
who tell you the intimate details of their sex-lives
but they would be shocked if you asked them how
much money they make. Society's unwritten pro-
hibition against speaking of the old spondulicks
belies the fact that, except for TV viewing, maxi-
mizing your moolah has become our country's
number one indoor sport. We think a lot about
money, we read magazines devoted entirely to it,
but publicly we still pretend it's filthy lucre.

My family didn't have any money to discuss,
so I never learned how impolite it was to bring up
the subject. That turned out to be a blessing. After
college I went to work in the methods and systems department of a large insurance company.
There I was at last, in the big city and in a real
job. I was putting in forty hours a week and another three hours a day commuting. My pay was
eighty dollars a week, and I was happy. Eighty
dollars wasn't a bad starting salary for an English
major with "no marketable skills" in 1963. I was
so enraptured with feeling like an adult, and so
glad to be earning some money at last, that I didn't
think much about whether I was worth more. I
didn't even know that 1963 was also the year Con-
gress passed the Equal Pay Act.

My one big gripe on the job was that there were no interesting men about. My college sweetheart had gone off to become an accountant without me, and I was lonely. The young men in my group were nerds. (The word "nerd" didn't exist then, but the species sure did.) One particularly repulsive one named Ben took a shine to me. My family did teach me to be sensitive to other people's feelings and not hurt anyone unnecessarily, so when he asked me to lunch, I hid all signs of nausea and said yes. That lunch changed my attitude about salaries.

Maybe he was preparing me for a proposal of marriage, more likely he just had nothing else to brag about. I'll never know why he did it, but before they even brought the stuffed clams *alla casa*, Ben started to tell me about his financial prospects. By his first anniversary with the company, he expected to receive a 10 percent raise. "That," he said, "will bring my salary to $99 a week." I don't know what he said after that. I was too busy figuring out that, although we started at the same time and were doing the same work, he was getting ten dollars a week more than I was. What made that even more provoking was that he did less work than I did and didn't do it as well.

With no previous instructions from my parents to go on, I said, "Do you mean that you earn ninety dollars now?" He confirmed my suspicions, and when I told him that I earned only eighty, he said "Oh, didn't you know? They pay men ten dollars a week more than they pay girls." To tell you the truth, I didn't get upset about the word "girls." It wasn't until a few years later that

Betty Friedan and Gloria Steinem pointed out that problem to me, but . . . you see, I grew up with three brothers and no sisters. I helped cook dinner, set the table, and washed and dried the dishes. They took turns taking out the garbage. I learned to be sensitive to sex discrimination way before I ever read the term in the paper. In fact, the power of my emotional response to Ben's news was probably rooted in experiences I had before I could even read. My fairness alarm went off.

After lunch, I complained to Barbara, my supervisor, about my pay being lower than Ben's. She told me those were company rules and she had nothing to do with salary policy. She agreed the pay scales were not fair, but she suggested that our only recourse was to work hard and try to earn raises if we needed more money. I've already told you I didn't learn about corporate etiquette at the family dinner table. Not realizing what a momentous step I was taking, I went to see Bill Moran, our section head. Bill had a handsome, kind, Irish face and a great sense of humor. I wasn't afraid of him. Besides, family life had taught me that if Mom says no, ask Dad.

Although I had never heard of the Equal Pay Act, Bill may have known about it. He listened to my protestations and took everything I said very seriously. There followed a series of urgent meetings with personnel people and upper management. I heard about the new law for the first time when the personnel manager asked me if I intended to invoke it. I said I wanted to be treated fairly; that was all. In the end they raised not only my salary but the salaries of every woman in the group to conform to what they were paying the men. I got a special bonus: Ben got mad at me, and he never asked me to lunch again.

That was the first raise I ever got by asking for it. The experience made me optimistic. Maybe you haven't been so lucky. Maybe you feel, as many people do, that asking for a raise is a waste of time. Our salaries are the reason we go to work, yet they are the part of our work-life over which we have least control. In fact, many people aren't even sure how their salaries are administered and a surprising number are as ignorant of their rights today as I was in 1963. Except for union members who have contracts to tell them what they will get, we are overwhelmingly in the dark about what we can expect in this important aspect of our lives. Many Americans are working very hard and still having trouble paying their bills.

Money problems are a major cause of stress-related disease. One study showed that the two leading causes of stress on the job were low pay and the absence of promotions or raises. In an eight-year study, researchers found that "economic stress" was an important predictor of the development of disease. This suffering is unnecessary. Some economists feel that much of the working population has been undervalued. Many people are just not paid what they're worth.

DO PEOPLE WORK
JUST FOR MONEY?

Theorists on motivation have muddied the monetary waters by claiming that people are not motivated by money. In a sense, they are right; most people know they are going to get paid a certain amount almost no matter what. On a day-to-day basis, it isn't the thought of a big raise that makes you work harder than you have to. If your performance is outstanding, your next raise isn't going to be that much higher than what you would get for average performance. For most people the difference after taxes is just a few dollars a week. No matter what they say about merit raises, nobody busts his hump for the price of a pepperoni pizza a week. We strive harder at work to satisfy other needs, not just to get a paycheck. But the bare fact is that no matter how psychologically rewarding we find our work, most of us wouldn't show up to do it if we didn't get paid.

Professors of management seek to convince managers of the importance of praise, self-esteem, and self-fulfillment; they want managers to know that people work for more than just money. I have no quarrel with that. My problem is that we are getting so distracted talking about so-called "intangible" rewards that we forget to make sure that people are paid enough. The secretaries who work for those professors and type those treatises about worker alienation can't afford to send their kids to college. Tellers in banks can't qualify for loans, nurses can't afford to get sick, and the man who cleans up in the theater can't afford a ticket to see the show. One year, on National Secretaries Day, that hideous invention of the florists' association, I saw a sign that said, "Raises, not Roses." Exactly right. If you get paid decently, you can afford to buy your own flowers, if that's what you want.

The proof of what I am saying is in an event that happens thousands of times every day. Disgruntled employees go out into the job market and almost inevitably get job offers at higher salaries. If they are worth more to the competition, why is it they can't get a few more simoleons from their current employers? One computer operator told me he went to a job interview with the salary he wanted in mind—20 percent more than he was making. When he got the job, they offered him 35 percent more. He wondered how long he'd been devaluing himself. I wondered what they had to pay his replacement.

The corporate response to all of this is to claim that companies can't afford to pay people more. In some instances this is correct. One thing we know, though, is that there is more money around for managerial raises than there is for nonmanagers. In 1985, for instance, executive raises in the United States averaged 7 to 8 percent compared with 4 percent for nonmanagers. It's all part of a common corporate policy that says if you have an orchard, we will be happy to give you an apple. Most disturbing is the trend toward huge bonuses for top executives. Effective leadership is rare, and it's not surprising that it doesn't come cheap. But a person should have to perform miracles to get seven or eight million dollars a year. And these big salary packages are often not tied to profit performance.

Worse yet are the golden parachutes, the huge severance packages given to executives who are leaving the company. In one case a CEO was paid seven million dollars in severance pay after only four months on the job. One wonders what he could possibly have done to earn it. And wouldn't the organization benefit more from giving incentive bonuses or decent raises to people who are going to stay on the job?

All this money going into the hands of top executives is supposed to motivate them to manage splendidly. Don't count on it. In one of my client companies, I'm certain that a big executive windfall cut into managerial efficiency, at least temporarily. The company was acquired by a large firm. I noticed in my work that many employees were fearful of the effects of the merger, and that morale was ebbing. The work force needed some attention from top management. I called the personnel manager to find out what they planned to do to smooth the transition and maintain employee productivity. He told me that the company's top managers had become very rich through the effect of the merger on their stock options. "Right now," he told me, "they're all too busy trying to shelter some of that income before the end of the tax year. And the people in personnel are running ragged trying to help them. But this won't last long. In another month or so we'll have them settled down."

I don't think he realized how outrageous that sounded to me. The executives' job was to take care of business. Morale was down and productivity was following it, but the executive board was busy meeting with tax shelter consultants. I bet the workers on the production line were not free

217

to make personal phone calls, much less attend to their finances during business hours. Wouldn't you love to know how that group of managers handled the budget for employee raises that year? If they did the usual thing for corporate managements, they kept it as low as possible.

WHY ARE
CHEAPSKATES CHEAP?

Managers are paid to keep costs down, so they postpone and minimize raises. Only a few smart companies pay their people as much as they can afford, instead of as little as they can get away with. Imagine if every organization adopted this policy: We want you to give us as much as you can so we're going to give you as much as we can.

Instead of being as generous as possible some bosses and some companies, for that matter, are just skinflints. They seem to be using pay scales that were in force in 1936.

Some think they should base raises on whether or not people need the money. Elise Olson, for instance, was a partner at a small brokerage house. She refused to give her secretary a raise. Matt Eisenberg worked for Elise and shared the same secretary, Jackie. Jackie complained to Matt about her lack of a raise. When Matt went to Elise to plead the secretary's case, Elise told him, "She just bought a new car and I saw her in here last month after lunch one day showing off her new Nettle Creek bedspread. Do you know what a Nettle Creek bedspread costs? If she can afford that and a new car, she doesn't need a raise."

Elise is a stockbroker. If you called her a Marxist, she'd have a stroke. But isn't that what her salary policy amounts to? I could be wrong, but from the little I learned in school about Marxism I remember the phrase, "From each according to his ability, to each according to his need." If I'm right, it would be fair to call people who make salary decisions on the basis of need Marxists. And to suggest that they also be paid on the basis of need.

In the capitalist system they tell us we work under, greater effort, not greater need, is supposed to bring greater rewards. If this is the rule, it should apply at all levels. Can you imagine anyone denying a department head or a CEO his raise because he doesn't need it? If he works for it, he expects to get it.

Which brings up an issue. You may be the cause of your boss's stinginess. Perhaps your boss sees your work as unworthy. Gutless bosses, who want to get rid of people, sometimes can't get up the courage to fire them. So they give them no raises and hope they'll quit. If you think your boss is holding back your raises, by all means check it out right away. I'd just get a few minutes alone with the boss and ask straight out, "It's occurred to me that your refusing to give me a raise might be your way of sending me a message. What are you trying to tell me?" Your tone needs to be right. Work on it so you won't sound smart-alecky, but get the idea out in the open. Even if you get bad news, you're better off dealing with it and moving on.

Whatever is going on with your salary, you can better understand, plan, and respond if you know the rules for salary administration in your company. In some small, owner-managed businesses, the rules are still capricious and arbitrary. If you work in such a place, you may find the fitful salary decisions confusing and frustrating. But remember this: When the company doesn't have an elaborate salary system, you can have more influence on what you get. Situations that are changeable are also more malleable.

In most large organizations, however, there are byzantine procedures for salary administration. There are a few reasons for this. Laws regulating salaries require employers to show that they give equal pay for equal work and that they do not discriminate against protected groups when they dole out the raises. Those laws, which supposedly protect us from unfair practices, turned out to be the full employment act for personnel salary administrators and salary system consultants. As a result of the work of these people, nowadays most large organizations have similar salary programs. They adopt the kind that keeps them out of trouble with the government. How fortunate for them that these same systems also tend to keep them out of trouble with their employees. You see, once a company has a system in place, managers can just point to the rules and put off any employee who has the audacity to ask for a raise. We are, however, not going to let that stop us. We are going to understand how these systems work and make sure we get everything we deserve from them.

HOW SALARIES ARE SET

Here is a general description of how one very common system works. (This one is called a point-factor system. The one in your company may differ slightly.) To begin with, salaries in any company are based on a couple of market measures: what other companies in the area and what other companies in the industry pay for similar work. Often organizations share information about what they are offering as starting salaries in certain common job categories. Some people see this practice as wage fixing, which they deplore as they would price fixing. As of now, however, I know of no laws that restrict companies from this practice.

Some firms also have job evaluation systems in which a committee reviews written descriptions of new or changed jobs. Points are given for various activities included in the job. The more complicated or difficult the activity, the more the points. Salaries are then set based on the number of points given to the job. Often, companies look at both this type of job evaluation and the market value when setting the salary.

Once a salary is set for a job, some companies have a simple system that budgets a pool of money for raises and gives considerable leeway to department heads on how they will distribute the money. Others exert more centralized control over how raises are doled out. Many organizations set what they call a minimum, midpoint, and maximum salary for that job. Then, theoretically, no one who does the job should get less than the minimum nor more than the maximum salary. These figures change when market conditions change. Or, in periods of high inflation, they may be raised as the cost of living goes up.

From here the salary administration formula in many companies goes like this. Starting salary for a given person depends on his or her qualification for the job: education and job experience. Raises depend on two things: the results of performance appraisal and where the person is in the salary range. The appraisal part is usually pretty straightforward. In companies that have this sort of system, there is usually a performance appraisal form that the bosses fill out once a year for each employee. From the performance appraisal form, the employee gets a rating, such as outstanding or above average. (You already know from chapter four how I feel about this; I won't go into it again here.) Anyway, the performance rating dictates what percentage of salary the employee will get in a raise. For instance, let's say Neville Numbquist and Clara Kleverski are both assistant string savers at the Mammon Manufacturing Company. Their boss, Farnsworth Fairbones, gives Neville an overall rating of "average." If Mammon Manufacturing has a system like the one we are describing, Neville would be entitled to a raise of, say, 5 to 7 percent. If Farnsworth rates Clara's work as "outstanding," Clara would be entitled to a raise of, say, 8 to 10 percent.

Now if Mammon Manufacturing also has salary ranges with minimums, midpoints, and maximums, we need to look at where Neville and Clara are in the salary range.

Let's say the salary range for assistant string savers is minimum—$200, midpoint—$264, and maximum—$327. If Neville is making $220, he is below the midpoint and would qualify for the higher percentage raise of 7 percent; he gets a $15.40 raise. If Clara, on the other hand, is already making $300, she is above the midpoint and can receive only the lower percentage raise of 8 percent. She gets a $24 raise. Also in this case, Clara's salary is now almost at the maximum for her job. Unless the company decides to raise the range, Clara won't get any more raises, no matter how well she does her job.

To many people, this sort of system sounds impossibly complicated. No one can deny that it is pretty intricate. It is meant, as we have said, to make sure companies comply with the law and keep central control over salary levels. Some cynics see these rules and policies as a way of keeping employees from asking for raises. If every time you try to hit the boss up for an increase, he starts giving you lectures about midpoints and minimums, you may just stop asking.

THERE IS ROOM TO MANEUVER

You may see these systems as airtight, but there are ways to influence them. Here's what you need to do:

First, learn as much as you can about the way salaries are administered in your company. The more you know about the system the better your chances of getting what you want from it.

This may seem trite, but in most places you really can earn slightly higher raises by making sure your boss admires your work. Now be careful. I did not say by working harder. You can do that, certainly. But the key here is that your boss has to notice what you are doing and approve of it enough to write about it on your appraisal form. With some bosses, you need to make sure they like you, because, of course, they can write anything they like on the piece of paper to make you look good if that's what they think you are. Chapter four gave you advice about how to communicate with the boss and how to make sure that your performance appraisal is handled properly. Go to it.

Another major place where you can influence the system is in the evaluation of your job. We said earlier that salary levels are set based on the complexity of the job. If your job has become more difficult or more responsible since you first took it, you may be able to convince your boss to have it upgraded. You do this by writing down what you are required to do, emphasizing work that requires independent judgment or special training. Ask your boss what you need to do to submit your job description for reevaluation. If you can get your job upgraded, you may or may not get a raise immediately, depending on your current salary and the new range. But the higher midpoint and maximum may make a difference in your next raise.

Let's go back to the case of Clara Kleverski.

You may recall that after her last raise, Clara was at the maximum for her job, so we know she can't get another raise as long as she stays in that job. But suppose Clara realizes that, since she now has to generate computer records of string saved, her job is more complex than it used to be. She follows my advice and asks Farnsworth to review her job to see if it should be upgraded. He agrees. Later, Farnsworth tells Clara her job now rates a minimum of $300, a midpoint of $376, and a maximum of $430. As a result, at her next salary review, Clara will not only be eligible for a raise, she will qualify for a higher one because her current salary is now below the midpoint of the new range. Most likely, though, she would not get a raise right away, since her salary is already higher than the new minimum. This next part may not seem fair, but through Clara's efforts Neville would probably get another $65 immediately. You may remember that just after his last raise, old Nevvy was getting only $235.40. With the increased range for the job, he is now below the minimum salary. So we have this weird situation. In a system designed to be fair, Clara the outstanding performer works to get her job upgraded and winds up getting no raise immediately. But her coworker, who is rated average, gets a big boost. The system doesn't always seem sane, but it does follow its own peculiar logic.

ASK ANYWAY

Regardless of how hopeless you think the prospects are, I urge you to ask for a raise if you think you deserve one. Even if your boss puts you off, at least she'll know what you expect, and she can take that into consideration next time she does her salary review. This is definitely a case of nothing ventured, nothing gained. Marcela Greenwald found that out by experience.

Marcela is such a nice and energetic person, I hate to call her middle-aged; but given the life expectancy of Americans, I guess she is. Marcela works hard and expects the company will take care of her. Most of the time she's been right, but for a while they seemed to forget to do that. You see, she had been working as an assistant to two lawyers in the firm where she worked. She also did some general office work. Her supervisor was the office manager, who made sure Marcela got regular raises. Then, one of the senior partners needed extra help. He asked for and got Marcela, and he was delighted to have her. She started working for him half time, then about thirty hours a week. Finally, he asked to have her assigned to him full time. She was glad he liked her work so much, enjoyed what she was doing, and liked the status of working with a full partner. When it came to raise time, though, she was disappointed. Her boss called her into his office, told her what a good job she was doing, and gave her a $1,000 a year raise. Under ordinary circumstances she might have been happy with that, but this time she was not.

When her husband Ken picked her up for the long drive home, she was visibly disturbed. He had to drag the bad news out of her. She acted as if she had done something wrong. In fact, she felt ashamed to tell him that she had not gotten the raise she thought she deserved. "A thousand dollars wouldn't be bad," she said, "but not after I've waited for eighteen months for an increase."

At first her husband tried to convince her that she should tell her boss she was disappointed. Ken was a manager in a clothing manufacturing firm, and he knew that if he had a good employee like Marcela, he would want to know if she was upset. Marcela never seemed to listen to what he was saying. She muttered and complained all the way home, and by the time they got there she was completely livid. She burned the carrots and said almost nothing during dinner.

By the next morning her attitude had changed. Without giving Ken any credit for thinking of it first, she announced that she was going to tell her boss how she felt. The rest of the trip to town was taken up with what Ken easily recognized as rehearsal. When he called her at lunchtime, she still hadn't brought up the subject with her boss; but that evening Ken could see her smile half a block away from where he picked her up.

"He didn't even know I hadn't gotten a raise last year," she said instead of saying hello. "He immediately went to see the office manager. She thought he had taken care of me last year, and he thought she had done it. When they found out that nobody had, they doubled my raise." They spent the rest of the trip planning a vacation.

Marcela's story has a nice ending, but there is a problem in it for me. She should have said something six months before. The generosity of her raise was fine but couldn't really make up to her for the money she "lost" while her boss straightened out who was in charge of reviewing her salary. Some people still think that all they have to do is work hard and wait for someone to notice. You'll be a wallflower for a long time if you wait for somebody to ask you to do the salary waltz. In times of rising prices, unless you get raises that at least match the inflation rate, you are losing ground. In a sense, you never really recover.

Certain groups tend to be underpaid. One study concluded that clerical workers were underpaid by 40 percent. Every study team from the National Academy of Sciences to Nine to Five, a secretaries' union, has concluded that the more women there are in an occupation, the less it pays. Strangely enough, the same occupations are often the most stressful. It seems fair that people who are going to have to put up with more strain should also experience more gain. Some people deal with their unbearable bosses by exacting higher wages. Jerks should have to pay more to get people to work for them.

HOW TO ASK FOR A RAISE

If you're going to get up your courage to ask for a raise, you're going to have to get rid of your old programming that tells you that you are being selfish or money-grubbing. Those feelings stand in the way of your getting what you deserve. If you don't really deserve a raise, don't ask for one. But if you do, go ahead and make your demands. You can do it without being overly aggressive or brassy.

Plan your campaign. As we have said before, your greatest asset will be a thorough knowledge of your organization's official salary policies. This information ought to be easily obtainable from your supervisor or the personnel department. Some companies still print the rules covering pay in their employee handbooks. (This practice, however, has gone out of fashion. Lately the courts have been ruling that statements made in employee handbooks can be considered terms of employment. Judges have, on several occasions, forced employers to abide by their own stated policies.)

Find out what you can about what they pay other people who do the same work. This may be difficult. Although many consider it an unfair labor practice, some companies still have policies against discussing salary. The real deterrent to your getting this information, however, will not be a corporate policy but the societal taboos against asking people such questions. Most of us just don't have the nerve to walk up to a colleague and say, "By the way, how much money do you make?" Close friends in the organization may be your best bet. One group of secretaries anonymously wrote their salaries on index cards and put them in a box. One of them made a recap for everyone to use.

You can also look at the figures published by the government. The Federal Bureau of Labor Statistics has average salary figures in different job categories. The most accessible numbers will be in the want ads in the local newspaper. (I wonder how many of you will look there to see if you should ask for a raise and wind up finding a new job. How silly employers are for not taking care of employees!)

Ask for a specific amount of money. Once you have the information you need, don't just ask for a raise. Mention a reasonable figure, one that fits the corporate guidelines if there are such things, but an amount you feel brings you into line with what others are making or rewards you for your superior contribution.

Give your boss a rationale for giving you a raise. Base your appeal on business judgment, not on your financial situation. We don't want them to dole out raises on their perceptions of what we need, so we can't use need as our reason. That's not the way it's done in this country. Use the data you have collected on what is generally paid for similar work in your area or your company. Cut out the ads from the newspaper and show them to the boss.

Document your contribution to the work group. Be ready to give the boss a brief rundown of successful projects you've done since your last raise. If your job has become more demanding, have some data handy on just how and when it changed. If you have taken the initiative to make yourself or your group more efficient, remind the boss of what you did. Bring in the thank-you notes you've received from other people, especially from customers.

Plan a matter-of-fact presentation. It may make you uncomfortable to have to remind the boss of how good you are at your job; but it will be worth it if it means you will be able to afford more nice outings with your family, or maybe just to pay the rent and meet the car payments.

Stick to your accomplishments when you develop your rationale. Talk about what you have done, rather than what others have failed to do. No matter how you resent others who are not pulling their weight, this is no time to vent that section of your spleen. You want to give the boss only positive images of you and your work.

Mention that you want to maintain your motivation. It is fair to come right out and say it: "A raise now will help me maintain my high level of dedication to my job. It will show me that you and the company appreciate my contribution. That will make me more satisfied with the job and keep me going."

Timing is important. Approach the boss before your regular salary review is due. If you wait until afterward, there may be nothing your boss can do to change a raise that has just been approved. If you get there ahead of time, at least your boss will know what you expect. It may influence her when she makes her recommendation.

Make your appointment with the boss and tell him you want to talk about your salary. Unless your boss is a super skinflint, it will be better for you if he knows what you want to talk about. Set up the meeting in the conference room if you can. It may make you feel more comfortable than trying to do this on the boss's turf.

AT THE MEETING

Keep a professional demeanor. Stay calm, but be assertive. Try to imagine that you are discussing the department's budget, not something so personal. It will help you enormously if you have planned in advance what you want, why you think you deserve it, and how you will react to the boss's responses. As you enter the meeting, picture yourself coming out with a big smile on your face, proud of how you conducted yourself, and triumphant about your boss's response. Keep those negative images of the boss's response out of your mind or you might inadvertently make them come true.

Use the supportive communication techniques from Chapter four. Be persistent. If the boss tries to interrupt you and put you off, ask for her patience. You can just say, "Marge, I have just a few more things I want to tell you. I promise to be brief, but I put a lot of thought into what I was going to say today, and I'd like an opportunity to finish." Then BRIEFLY complete what you were going to say. If you are one of those people who talks too much when you're nervous, watch how long you go on. If there's a clock in the room where you are meeting, sit where you will face it. It will help you stay on schedule.

Stay calm, no matter what your boss's response. Make no threats. You may be forced to carry them out. If your boss refuses your request, ask why. You might say, "It will help me accept your decision if I know exactly why you are saying no."

If you get turned down, ask for advice. If you think your boss is just putting you off by saying, "Now is not the time," be gracious and find out when will be the right time. Then, when you come back at the time the boss suggests, you will have the advantage. In fact, at that point, you will begin by saying, "Four months ago when I came to ask you for a raise, you suggested that this month would be the best time for us to talk about it." It will make it sound as if you are only following orders.

If your boss tells you she doesn't have the authority to grant you a raise, ask her for permission to talk to the person who does. Also ask her if she agrees that you deserve a raise. Say you would like to tell the person in authority that your boss supports you in this.

If your boss turns you down because he thinks you don't deserve a raise, ask what you have to do to make yourself eligible. Then you can weigh his demands. If it's worth it to you, you may want to improve your work performance and strengthen your case for next time.

Ask for other kinds of compensation if there is no way you can get a raise. To many of us these days, time off from the job to pursue other interests is as important as a few extra dollars a week. Perhaps there is a conference coming up that you would like to go to at company expense, or a course you would like to take. These things cannot really compensate you for "lost" income, but they may be the best you can get for now.

End on a congenial note. Whatever you decide to do ultimately, you are going to have to work with that boss a little longer. Why not make it as pleasant as possible?

THERE ARE LAWS
TO PROTECT YOU

Wage and hour laws, like employee safety and antidiscrimination laws, are on the books. They are
there to protect you. But do they? Well, yes and
no. Many employers get away with illegal practices because employees are reluctant to sue. Few
employees even know what laws there are. To the
extent that these laws work, they do so mostly by
scaring employers. Fear of lawsuits frightens them
into doing what they should have the good business sense to do anyway—treat their employees
fairly.

If you feel your employer is violating the law,
you may want to begin by asking your boss if such
and such a law applies to you. Veiled threats have
been known to work. They may, shall we say, encourage your employer into compliance.

In an extreme case, you may want to talk to a
lawyer or your state labor board to see if you should
sue for your rights. I say "in an extreme case" because, as you probably realize, such lawsuits are
emotionally draining and time-consuming. It may
be worth your while if the payoff is substantial. I
don't mean that we should allow the law to be
broken and do nothing about it. Realistically,
though, I must warn you that legal action may not
be worth it.

If you work for a total cheapskate, you may
just be better off leaving and going to work for
someone who is smart enough to pay you what
you're worth.

10

BLOWHARDS AND EGOMANIACS

*Pride, Envy, and Avarice are
the three sparks that have
set these hearts on fire.*

Dante Alighieri
The Divine Comedy

All bosses have egos. The problem is that some have egos that expand to fill the space available. You can barely get into a room with them without bumping into their vainglory. Narcissism is a troublesome trait in anyone. In a boss, it's enraging. Ask Rosa Chang. She works for one of the great strutting roosters of the American Southwest. Ron Nash rose through the ranks to the number two position in an investment company. In his early years, he knew the market, made some really smart decisions, and became the golden-haired boy in the firm. He could do no wrong, or so they all thought; and so, unfortunately for Rosa, he still believes.

When Rosa, right out of grad school, took the job working for Ron, she was certain that it was the opportunity of a lifetime. As Ron's research assistant, she would do a lot of the legwork for the deals he was making, be party to all of his decision-making, and help him evaluate investments. In other words, she would learn to think the way he thought, to make money the way he did. She was on her way to getting rich.

Rosa was right about one thing. She learned a lot in that job. She learned how to deal with a powerful man who sincerely believed he was always right. She learned patience and humility, and she learned them from a man who had neither.

Her first lesson came from Ron's compulsion to check over everything that went out of his department. Rosa had been an excellent student. She considered herself intelligent and independent enough to handle the lesser details on her own. Yet simple letters had to wait to be mailed so Ron could make sure they were right and sign them himself. He made superficial changes in the wording. No amount of pleading convinced him that Rosa was capable of writing and signing her own letters. She tried to persuade him on the basis of the backlog this created. Ron was unconcerned about the extra work for the secretaries and the delays. He controlled everything, and that's the way he wanted it.

One day in early 1985 Rosa brought Ron a proposal that the firm sell its interest in an oil exploration company. She was sure that oil prices had to start dropping soon. Ron took one look at the recommendation on the first page and tossed the whole report in the wastebasket. He never even read the rationale. When she asked him what he wanted to do, he said, "You're young Rosa. This sort of proposal is a good exercise, but you can't expect me to take advice from you."

Three months later at the quarterly review, it became obvious that Rosa had been right. They had to sell, and at a much lower price. No one mentioned that Ron had ignored Rosa's recommendation. As was usually the case with Ron, being wrong made him act insulted. He ranked out Rosa and stormed out of the room.

Little by little, Rosa began to buy into the game Ron was playing. He ignored any information that didn't fit in with his preconceived ideas, so she stopped telling him things she knew he'd reject. Soon her reports played down problems and emphasized the rightness of his past decisions. As she watched the profit picture begin to slide, Rosa realized that she was contributing to the decline by whitewashing issues. She decided she couldn't let herself become a coward. Now she's looking for another job, but she's still holding information back from Ron. "He yells at me," she says. "Why should I take abuse from him in order to save his investments? I'm getting out so I don't really care what happens to him. I'm just keeping calm and waiting for a job offer."

In some ways the relationship has been good for Rosa. She is bitter that her ideas have been ignored, but she admits that Ron's scorn has burned her arrogance out of her. She can keep her temper under battle conditions, a skill she's sure to need in the investment business. She knows how to deal with an elephantine ego. She's bound to run into a few more of those along the way.

HOW TO SPOT A BONEHEADED PEACOCK

By all reports Albert Einstein was a humble man. He didn't criticize others. He asked colleagues to have patience with him because, he said, he didn't understand things quickly. When he worked with a group, he came across as an equal. If you're that smart, perhaps you don't have to worry if anyone is noticing how important you are.

The egomaniacal among us are the opposite of Einstein. They are impatient, judgmental; they hog the credit, and, often, they aren't very smart. What they are good at inventing is creative ways to serve their voracious appetites for self-satisfaction. They become so preoccupied with making a name for themselves that they are blind to obvious practical issues.

Wendy Sacal, for instance, is a process engineer in a chemical plant. She devised what she considered a breakthrough in producing a chemical fertilizer that was one of her firm's most promising new products. Her idea was, in fact, a good one. Her boss Judd Baird gave her the go-ahead to implement her idea. The problem was that she got so engrossed in her new method that she ignored the feelings of the other people who had to be involved in making her idea work. When she explained her process at a meeting, she used a lot of technical terms and drew a lot of molecules on the blackboard. It sounded like double-talk and looked like chicken wire to her audience, but she went along oblivious to their confusion. When they didn't show much enthusiasm for her idea, it never occurred to her that they didn't understand her. She told herself they were jealous of her technical brilliance. She stopped trying to get them to admire her work.

In the end, the idea was implemented, but not with the increased productivity Wendy had predicted. Some of the efficiency was lost because the people who ran the plant never really understood her method. But those people were not only ignorant, they were also unenthusiastic. They didn't sabotage Wendy's idea, but they didn't go out of their way to increase the glory she was so obviously pursuing.

Like many egoists before her, Wendy's preoccupation with herself, her career, and her own ideas blinded her to the practical considerations so vital to her own success. Conceit causes people to form opinions based on gossip and wishful thinking, to voice criticism without looking at the facts, and to focus on petty issues at the expense of important concerns. They quarrel about who is right instead of concentrating on solving the problem at hand.

These know-it-all bosses may just be afraid to appear ignorant to underlings. They may be convinced managers are supposed to know everything, so they pretend they do. Others seem genuinely convinced they do know more than anyone. Whatever the reasons for their behavior, they wreak havoc.

The political rat's nest is the natural habitat of egomaniacal managers. They are vague and subjective in measuring their employees' performance. Their people, therefore, are left to try to gain acceptance and approval by cozying up to the boss rather than by doing excellent work. Employees jockey for position and work to impress the manager, often at the expense of getting the job done. This can lead to cliquishness and vindictiveness. Employees begin to compete with one another for the boss's favor. They give their loyalty to the individual manager, not to the organization. All this feeds the boss's ego, but not the corporate coffers.

Some egotists prefer sultanhood, enjoy being surrounded by their admiring minions. Others like to rule from the top of the mountain. From inside the closed doors of the office, with the framed motto "Familiarity Breeds Contempt" on the wall, they practice management by memo. Without consulting the people who will be affected, they formulate policy and issue sovereign edicts. These icemen may be technically competent and important contributors in their own right, but since they do not communicate person-to-person with their people, they fail to elicit real commitment from them.

Managers can have some pretty misguided notions about what they are due. Louise Hanley worked for one such deluded demagogue. Louise was a secretary in a sportswear manufacturing firm. Her boss, Matt Franklin, was motivated by his own urgent need for personal comfort. He seemed to think that being the boss meant that all the other people in his department were his servants. Louise resented his demands but she wasn't quite sure what to do about them. She didn't want to seem petty about what she was and wasn't willing to do, but sometimes his requests were outrageous. The worst was the bell system. No, not the phone company; I mean the system Matt installed to call Louise into his office. He buzzed her from his desk. One ring meant he wanted her to bring him a cup of coffee; two rings meant he wanted her to take dictation; three rings meant she should bring the coffee and her dictation pad. He would ring the bells, and Louise would think about wringing his neck.

Perhaps if Louise had told Matt that she resented the bells he would have found another way to communicate what he wanted. But she never explained her feelings to him. She was convinced that he was too much of a know-it-all to listen to anything she had to say. Louise might have been wrong about Matt, but her instincts were right about egotists in general. They often think they are omniscient. And, thinking they know everything, they find no reason to listen to anyone else. Perhaps egomania has a chemical cause that also affects a person's hearing.

On the other hand, egotists have no trouble talking. Unaware of the effect of their bombast on those around them, they spew forth long words and intricate sentences that mean very little to anyone but them. They "discuss the merits of subjecting the product to elevated temperature conditions" when they mean they want to see if cooking the soup will solve the problem.

Blowhard bosses often have posture problems. They lean back in their chairs, put their feet up on the desk, and act generally distracted while you are trying to tell them how to improve the department's bottom line. They can't seem to think about anything but themselves.

All this attention to detail must be very tiring. If so, that would explain why some managers can't move around much. They sit at their desks and shout orders or information at their employees. Barb Paskin worked for one woman who would sit in her office and call out criticisms—"Barb, this invoice is wrong. How could you make such a dumb mistake?"—loud enough for the whole department to hear.

Many of these managers are inordinately concerned with status symbols—titles, the size of their offices, who else has a window. June Natale got her Ph.D. and it seems as if she changed her first name to "doctor." She wouldn't let anyone call her anything else. Otto Strozer was only thirty-two. He called his sixty-year-old secretary "Ruth," but he insisted that she call him "Mister."

THEY WORRY ABOUT THE WRONG THINGS

People who have real self-confidence don't have to spend their time worrying about who has a bigger expense account or a taller plant in his office. Faced with real injustice they take steps to redress their legitimate grievances, but they don't go around looking for slights and snubs that don't exist. They get their satisfaction from doing the job well. They take care of business.

Self-seeking bosses, on the other hand, don't find the time to spend with their subordinates. They like to be called managers, but they resent the needs of their people. They prefer to spend all their time trying to impress their own bosses. If someone with power calls, they abandon their people and run.

Given the choice, the manager with a "pasha complex" will have his employees do his personal errands and ignore their real work. One boss made his secretary feel like a fool by insisting that she look up a word in the dictionary so he could finish his crossword puzzle. If you can ignore such power plays and get the job done, good for you. More likely, they will give you permanent indigestion. And imagine what they cost the organization in lost efficiency.

EFFECTS OF EGOMANIA

Effort that should be directed toward the organization's goals is wasted on serving the boss's ego. Instead of working on high priority projects, employees attend to trivialities. These bosses sacrifice real success for petty satisfactions.

Employees who work for such bosses also suffer personal losses. It isn't just the frustration and outrage. These take a serious health toll on some people. But on top of the emotional losses, employees learn little, careers stall, and workers have no sense of accomplishment. Other managers may recognize blowhards for the fools they are, and those who are loyal to them may be guilty by association. Who would be loyal to a jerk but another jerk?

Ray Reynolds took a long time to come to this conclusion. When he and I had our last conversation about Warren Kramer, Ray had just left Kramer Realty to, in his own words, "go to work for a real company."

Warren started the realty company that bore his name, and he succeeded. He was brilliant at real estate. Nobody denied that, not even Ray when he had quit after eleven years with the firm. Everyone in the company also knew that no one worked harder than Warren did. He was a multimillionaire; but he was in the office early every day, and he stayed late. In fact, if his employees were going to complain about anything in this regard, they would say they wished Warren would slack off a little. Leave them alone to do their jobs.

You see, Warren thinks he has to be involved in everything. For instance, he hired Margaret Mishima to do the firm's advertising. Margaret was highly qualified and got a good salary. But Warren never left her alone. Ray said, "Margaret was in my office every day complaining about the boss." She would tell me how she would get her advertising all worked out, and Warren would change it at the last minute.

"He comes in just before the deadline and starts meddling. He questions everything. In the end, we wind up with something very like what I had done in the first place," Margaret told Ray. "But then he thinks he did it. He comes into my office to rob me of the credit for my own work." Ray tried to soothe Margaret's feelings. She stayed with the firm for a while, but then she left. Warren seemed to have a knack for hiring highly motivated people and then alienating them.

And they all seemed to come to Ray for sympathy. Grace Williams, Warren's secretary, complained about the personal favors Warren demanded of her. Ray tried to tell her that those things were normal in a privately owned firm. But even Ray thought it was too much when Warren asked if Grace's husband would deliver a package. "My husband resents how much Warren imposes on me," she told Ray. "If he starts interfering with the rest of my family, I'll have to quit." Eventually she did.

When Ray first started to tell me these stories, I asked him why he stayed with the firm. He told me that Warren's antics didn't bother him that much. He just felt sorry for the rest of the people in the company. But Ray continued to tell me stories and became more and more emotional about them himself.

When I asked Ray what he could do to stop the nonsense, he absolutely rejected the idea of influencing Warren's behavior. "He's a manager with an open door and a closed mind," Ray told me. "It's no use trying to change him." Again I asked why Ray didn't consider going to another company. He said that Warren basically left him alone, and that he felt he earned more working for Warren than he could working elsewhere. He stayed.

The showdown finally came, not over Warren's bad treatment of good employees but over his misplaced loyalty to bad ones. Eventually Ray and I had a good laugh over what happened with the person he called Joe the janitor.

Joe was hired to clean the office and do errands (presumably the errands Grace's husband had refused to do). As was the case with many of the people Warren hired, Joe's duties were a bit nebulous. Everyone supposed that Joe was to clean the office and keep supplies stocked. But Joe knew exactly what to do. He washed Warren's car a lot. And drank. Several times a day the people from the office could see him from the front windows, walking up the hill to the local gin mill. In the meantime, the office was dirty and people wasted time looking for forms that should have been handy. Warren either didn't notice or looked the other way.

Then, one morning at 10:30, Ray went into the men's room. He heard snoring coming from one of the booths. He knocked on the door but got no answer. He looked under the door and saw Joe's scuffed, black shoes. What could Ray do? He went into the other booth, stood on the toilet and looked over the divider. There was Joe, fully clothed (thank goodness), sitting on the pot, fast asleep. And no amount of poking or yelling could rouse him.

Ray is a very tall man. He couldn't get the door to the booth open on his own. He had to go out to the computer area and get Steve, the five-foot-five computer operator, to help him. Steve crawled under the door of the booth, opened it and helped Ray drag Joe out. Eventually, they woke him up.

Ray went to Warren and told him the story. "The guy is a drunk, Warren. I know this is your company, but I think we have to get rid of him."

Warren said he thought Ray was being harsh. "Now there's no doubt he's had a few too many this morning, Ray, but I don't think you can call a person a drunk based on one incident."

"This isn't a single incident, Warren," Ray responded.

"Oh, come on, Ray. Joe does a lot of work for me around my house on weekends. I don't remember ever seeing him drunk." That was all Ray could get Warren to say.

After the men's room incident, Joe behaved himself for a while. He didn't do much work, but at least he didn't pass out in the office. Then the situation started to deteriorate. Soon Joe was, if not totally sloshed, at least slightly tipsy just about all the time. In his besotted state, he started to pinch the women who worked in the office. A little pat here, a little tweak there, and pretty soon everyone was putting her back to the wall as soon as Joe came by. Ray, of course, was the crying towel for all the ensuing complaints. He was about to organize a petition signed by all the employees to get rid of Joe when "The Great Fileroom Fracas" took place.

One Thursday afternoon, Sharon Murphy, a young agent with the firm, was in the file room bending over to get a property file out of a bottom drawer. When Joe entered the file room, Sharon's (*ahem*) back was to the door. Joe still must have been able to make out shapes through the bleary-eyed haze he traveled in. He lurched forward, right hand outstretched, palm first. Later Sharon couldn't recall whether she smelled or felt Joe first, but as soon as his hand touched her, she wheeled around and socked him. He went down like a dead tree in a hurricane.

Warren was out of the office and didn't hear about the battle until the next morning. He responded by transferring Sharon to another office and firing Joe.

Everyone was glad to see Joe properly dealt with at last, but they were angry about Sharon's transfer. True, she lost her temper, but not without provocation. But at least Joe was gone.

The following Monday, Warren, ignoring frivolous considerations like morale and productivity, decided that the whole incident was Sharon's fault. He hired Joe back. When Ray told me about this incident, he was furious. It was clear he had had enough of Warren's self-centered attitude and poor judgment. He promised me (himself, really) that he would clear up a few deals he was working on and go somewhere where he wouldn't have to be a constant witness to ego-blinded management.

Four months later, Ray had resigned. We had dinner together when he was taking a week off before he started his new job. He was ecstatic about having gotten out at last. His enthusiasm for his new association would boost his sales, I was sure. I asked him about several of his old coworkers that he had told me about over the years. He didn't know what had happened to Sharon. We speculated that she had gone on to win the Golden Gloves in Brown County. Most of the others were gone. Someday, I thought, that firm will consist of Warren and Joe, and no one else.

HOW TO HANDLE
THE PURE EGO BOSS

Lay in a good supply of kid gloves. If you are going to stick with the egocentric boss, you'll need them. You are going to have to put up with the boss's psychology, since you are highly unlikely to change it. You may be able to get the boss to do certain things that you think are essential, like allowing you the credit you deserve or giving you a chance to try out your own ideas. But you should expect that the boss will continue with certain annoying habits. Even if you get the boss to agree to give up certain of them, like answering the phone while you're having a meeting, he will probably, consciously or subconsciously, invent creative new ways to be insensitive.

Be as specific and concrete as possible when you discuss issues with such a boss. To maximize your chances of changing the boss's behavior, say exactly what you want. If you say, "I want you to show more respect for my contribution around here," your boss may not understand what you are talking about. You need to communicate in precise images. "When you asked me to put aside my analysis of the couponing program and go out to buy your husband a birthday present, it made me feel that my work around here is not very important. I want to feel that I am making a real con-

tribution, that my work is too vital to be interrupted with small, personal errands—mine or
anyone else's." It takes guts to be this specific, but
it will work better in the long run. Even if it doesn't
change the boss's habits, it will at least show you
to be a serious, motivated worker, not a lazy malcontent.

**Get other people's agreement to back up your
ideas.** For instance, if you want to add another
printer to the department's word processing system, get some expert support for your idea. Then,
instead of just making a recommendation on your
own, you can say, "Roger Shepherd from data
processing was saying at a meeting the other day
that they have guidelines on how many printers a
department might need. I found out the average
volume per printer in the company. Then, I looked
at what we're producing here. It seems our volume is high enough to warrant at least one more
machine."

Use a delicate touch with this. Don't give the
boss the impression that you went out to get ammunition to use against him. Make it sound more
casual than that. Also, take care that the idea comes
across clearly as your own. With this type of boss
you are going to have enough trouble getting the
credit you deserve. You don't want to go giving it
away voluntarily.

**Try selectively ignoring your boss's more im-
possible or stupid demands.** Steve Strieker works
in the Milan office of an international firm. During
a period of high inflation he tried to get his boss
to change the forms they used for financial report-

ing to headquarters in New York. The forms asked for dollars converted into the local currency, accurately reported to two decimal places. That made sense in Switzerland and Japan where small units of currency were significant parts of a dollar. But at the time a hundredth of a lira was equal to about five one-hundredths of a penny. He told his boss in New York that it made sense to drop the decimal places. His boss insisted that Steve follow the rules. But there just wasn't space in the columns for all the zeros that Steve was required to report. Steve knew his boss hated to be challenged. If he had pressed his point the boss would have gotten huffy. Steve did it the easy way. He just took it upon himself to report the equivalent of full pennies and drop the extra decimal places. His boss never noticed.

If your boss cares nothing for your ideas and your motivation, if she is so wrapped up in herself that you cannot achieve your own job satisfaction, you may have to go and find another boss. To survive in the meantime, you may have to forget about making a dent at all. You may just have to set your own ideas aside until you can plant them in more fertile ground than the hard, dry clay of your boss's brain.

Try to see the boss's offensive behavior as what it is, an aberration of his own personality and not reflective of your personal worth. Keep the stomach remedies handy. Jogging, yoga, or some other deep relaxation techniques may be the best antidote until you move on to a more benign environment.

11

THE MANAGER AS SOCIAL WORKER

The virtue most in request is conformity. Self-reliance is its aversion.

Ralph Waldo Emerson

E d Denton got to be a manager by being a professional good guy. After business school, he started in the management training program of a large electronics firm. From the beginning, the people he worked with loved him, and that's just the way he wanted it. He worked hard to make sure he pleased everyone, from the division heads to the porters. In his year and a half as a trainee, he rotated from department to department, staying in each one only three or four months. In his travels, he won many friends and influenced many people. They all concluded that he was just wonderful; but after three years with the firm, the honeymoon may finally be over.

Ed has a problem: His main objective as a manager is to make people like him. He gives his employees what they ask for and the ones who have the nerve to ask get a great deal—time off, trips to conventions, and special training programs. But they don't respect Ed very much. The ones who haven't the nerve to ask resent Ed's "playing favorites."

No matter how much they deserve it, Ed can't criticize his people, not even constructively. His performance appraisals follow Grandma's dictum: If you can't say anything nice, don't say anything at all. Ed says a manager's major concern must be morale. He wants his people to be happy. He fears making demands on them, so he avoids the subject of work. Instead he talks to them about their families and sports. If you asked him, he would tell you they are good, hardworking people, and that he doesn't need to push them. He hopes that by being supportive and sweet he will inspire them to be nice to him in return.

The strategy has backfired. Productivity is down because Ed refuses to make tough-minded demands on his people. Morale is also down because his employees want challenging work and a boss who will teach them things and help them grow. They are all hoping that top management will soon notice that they made a mistake in appointing Ed a manager.

If you have a boss like Ed, his super-friendly attitude probably enticed you into the job. But now you may be disappointed to find your work group has a social director instead of a leader. We all prefer a boss who is concerned about us as people; but we go to the plant, the hospital, or the office to do work, and we want someone to show us that what we do has value. Children play all day. We're adults; we want to feel our actions are important in themselves.

HOW DO THESE
CLUBBY PEOPLE GET
TO BE BOSSES?

Mostly, bosses in this category are chosen because they are so nice. They accept the job of manager, but authority makes them uncomfortable. So they hide from power. Otis MacDonald, for instance, had a very common, painful problem: He couldn't get used to the idea that he was a manager. He had started at the bottom. When he worked on the production line, he saw management as the enemy. He sat for hours with his friends complaining about the company executives, their ineptitude, their perks, their suits, their big cars. He was a foreman for a short time, and while he was out there on the floor he pretended he was still "one of the guys." Now he's in the front office and finds it hard to play the role of the "executive." He thinks his old buddies must be making fun of his white shirt and tie. He still identifies with them, which is fine, but he worries too much that his decisions will be unpopular. Instead of using his experience and his perspective to benefit everyone, he spends his time wondering what the people in his old work units are thinking of him.

Otis's feelings of ambivalence come from his inability to make the transition from worker to manager. He is uncomfortable with power. Some new managers are sent to training programs that enhance this discomfort. Certain so-called management development courses teach participants that because employees are less powerful, bosses should take care of them. This emphasis on the difference between being a manager and being an employee makes the managers feel guilty. They assuage their guilt by being too nice.

Other managers use being sweet to manipulate people into compliance. They know that folks have a hard time saying no to a nice guy. Sometimes they are right. One bank personnel manager told me that his organization had made the unlikely choice of appointing a nun to be a branch manager. I knew that these days, sisters did other things besides teaching in parochial schools, but I wondered how a member of the clergy functioned in a financial institution. It turned out Sister Anna was doing quite well. She always stuck to the rules and made sure her employees did the same, a very important issue in a bank. In her personnel decisions she tended toward helping hardship cases, but her faith in them paid off. Her people were loyal, hard working, and honest in a way we rarely see in today's world. In her case, the "social worker" approach worked. This is not always the case. Sometimes, overly concerned bosses annoy their people and get in the way of productivity.

BEHAVIORS OF BUDDY BOSSES

If your boss is more interested in how you feel than how the work is going, you may wonder what the boss's function is supposed to be. You will find it hard to take seriously anyone who calls himself a manager and gives the bowling banquet a higher priority than profitability.

Bosses who cast themselves in the role of "daddy" or "mommy" solve problems for people instead of teaching them to solve them for themselves. They cover up for their employees and, sometimes, they actually do the work themselves, especially if they consider it too difficult for the staff members to do. They don't help people recognize their shortcomings and overcome them. Instead, they compensate for them.

These managers often think they know what's best for people. Instead of allowing employees to make their own career choices and helping them grow naturally, super-concerned bosses pressure their people with the "father knows best" approach.

The boss with a faulty social conscience may exhibit it by being absolutely egalitarian. She will treat everyone alike despite the circumstances. She will shy away from rewarding or recognizing those who make a greater contribution. This will rob people of their incentive to do better.

Any good boss realizes that people with special problems may need to be given lighter loads temporarily. Some social worker bosses, however, carry this to extremes and allow malingerers to slough off their work onto the energetic and ambitious.

Extremely democratic managers also are often averse to disciplining employees. They may let their people go their own ways rather than taking the steps to keep them on course.

EFFECTS OF
MATEY MANAGEMENT

If the boss is paying more attention to who's happy than to who's producing, the bottom line will suffer. The initially pleasant atmosphere eventually degenerates and the effectiveness of the organization declines. It happened at a New England accounting firm that had the quintessential chummy chairman. The company employed 140 people; and before Bruce Rodgers took over, it had been run by a whip cracker who pushed people without regard to their human needs. Bruce swore he would do the opposite, and he did. He wanted to show everyone accounting could be fun. He wanted to prove that his predecessor was atypical. He just had to show every employee that he cared. In the end, the people felt more like members of a fraternity than employees of an important accounting firm.

Bruce decided that he wanted people to think of him not as a CEO but as a coach. He gave each office of the firm a "team identity"—the Boston Bears, the Providence Pelicans. He had insignia made for each group. He wore a baseball cap with the corporate logo on it to meetings and continually asked people whether they were having fun.

Eventually, his nutsy image became known outside the firm. Employees were embarrassed by his game show host public persona. They dreaded running into him in the halls when they had clients with them. The truly dignified among them quit. The silliness of the firm's sporty image lost the company several clients before Bruce was forced out in favor, unfortunately, of another slave driver. The old employees who are still there say the firm is schizophrenic, swinging back and forth between harshness and party time.

Bruce is a rarity. Since corporate productivity suffers under social worker management, we seldom find it at the highest levels. But lower down the organization, we see how it affects the individual employee.

COULD A BOSS THIS NICE BE BAD FOR YOU?

There's a difference between having a boss who cares about you and one who wants to take care of you. The former respects you, maybe likes you, as a human being. The latter sees you as someone who can't take care of himself. His attitude toward you is based on sympathy and pity. He wants to do for you all the things you can't do for yourself. This demeaning approach encourages you to be dependent. It prevents you from learning to stand on your feet, from feeling and using your own power and competence. It is insidious because it seems like selflessness but is actually the ultimate power trip. Without looking like a bad guy to himself or to anyone else, the boss can confirm his superiority and your inferiority. And you are supposed to be grateful for all he's done for you.

If you have a sense of your own power, if you want to feel your own independence, you will reject any boss's attempts to make you unduly dependent. You will find it demeaning if she makes your decisions for you. You will feel patronized and degraded. At first you may enjoy the absence of stress, the lack of responsibility, the hot tub of solicitousness. Eventually, though, many of us chafe at having a parental boss when we feel old enough to make our own decisions.

There is a difference between a boss who backs you up and one who covers up for you. In the first instance, you know you can count on your boss to stand by you when someone questions your decisions or attacks your work. In the latter, your boss does things for you, fixes your errors without telling you. By saving you from the consequences of your mistakes, he ensures that you never learn, never reach your full potential. Employees whose bosses do the work for them often end up out in the cold when the boss leaves the company. The new manager soon discovers that her predecessor has been harboring incompetents. The new broom could sweep you away.

If your boss starts to make your personal decisions as well as your business decisions for you, you could wind up like Al Portsman. When Al first graduated from high school, he went to work for a small manufacturing company that made cookware. The company was owned by Jerry Sloane, an elderly, gracious gentleman, but it was run by his son, Vincent. Vincent liked Al and took him under his wing. Al felt lucky that the owner's son liked him so much. Al did what he was told and felt secure that he would be taken care of. In fact, he used that term often when describing his boss. "He takes care of his people," Al said.

And Vincent did. He promoted Al from stock boy to supervisor of the storage area. He paid Al well and encouraged him. He told Al exactly what to do and expressed his gratitude when Al carried out his orders exactly. When the company expanded, he gave Al additional responsibilities for shipping and supplies. Al was a bright enough guy and learned to do his new job, except for one aspect of it. He never made any decisions. Whenever anything had to be decided, whether it was what color to paint the supply room or who should be assigned to take the mail to the post office, he asked Vincent what to do. And Vincent told him. And Al did just as he was told.

Eventually, Al began to take Vincent's advice about other kinds of decisions. When Al got married, Vincent advised him about where to look for an apartment. When Al bought his first house, Vincent told him where to go for his mortgage. When Al's first child was born, Vincent gave the boy a thousand dollar savings bond. Al named his son Albert Vincent.

Things went along like this for years. Al felt blessed. Sometimes he agreed with some of the other people at work when they criticized Vincent, but he felt he owed Vincent a great deal. One evening, Al and his wife Donna were driving home after having dinner with one of his colleagues, Kaye McKenna, the marketing director. "I think what Kaye said at dinner is right, Al," Donna said. "Sloane's designs need to be updated. These days gourmet cookware is coming in. They need to change their image, or they'll have trouble. If you don't believe me I'll show you what they're featuring in the latest Marshall Field's catalog."

"I know she's right about that, Donna, but she approaches him all wrong. And she wants me to fight with him the way she does. I just can't do it. Look at what he's done for us. I don't have a college degree. Where could I find someone who would give me such a high level job without one?" At that point, Al was in charge of operations for the whole company.

In the months that followed, Al sometimes had a nagging idea in the back of his mind that the others were right. Sales were starting to fall off a bit. When he mentioned it, Vincent said it was just a small economic downturn. It was affecting the whole country, not just them; but it was nothing to worry about. Al wanted to believe Vincent, so he did.

When Vincent heard about the expected arrival of Al and Donna's second child, he urged Al to look for a new house. He said, "You know, Al, you and your family have moved up in the world since you bought the house in East Millford. You should really look for a place in a better area, where your kids will go to school with better types of people."

Later, Al remembered that conversation as the beginning of the end for him. But at the time, it seemed like the beginning of the beginning. Al talked to Donna about the new house. At first she was reluctant to leave their home. She had lots of friends in the neighborhood and so did their son. Since she had quit her job after the first baby was born, the company of the other women in their area was important to her. She wanted to stay in their old house.

But when she started to go around with Al to look at bigger houses, she changed her mind. The places they saw were so lovely, the roads were winding, the lawns and backyards were larger, and the trees were bigger, older, so graceful. Donna loved those trees. They were nothing like the skinny little trees in their development. Eventually, they bought a new place.

The biggest surprise to them was that the higher interest rates really made their monthly payments a lot higher. Al mentioned that to Vincent. Vincent told him not to worry. The mortgage interest was tax deductible.

For a while, Al was very wrapped up in the new house and soon after that the new baby. He did his job as well as he could, of course, but he noticed the declining sales. His colleagues blamed the company's increasingly serious problems on Vincent, on his insistence that he be intimately involved in every decision, and on his refusal to modernize the company's product line. Vincent blamed their problems on the recession that was a daily topic in every newspaper.

When Kaye left the company she had a talk with Al and Donna. "I'm going someplace where I can weather this economic storm. I don't think Sloane's is going to do very well in the next year or so. You ought to consider getting out." Donna agreed with Kaye. Al didn't say much until after Kaye went home. Then he told Donna how he felt. "I think she may be right, but I don't see how I can just leave. She's got a degree in marketing. She can go to a bank or an insurance company and get a good job. I never even took one college course. No other company would even interview me for a job at my level. I'd have to take a cut in pay. And you know we can't afford that. Our mortgage payments are too big."

They decided to try to stick it out. Donna vowed that in a year or so, when the new baby was old enough to go to a sitter, she would look for a job. In the meantime, they would be as frugal as possible.

During the next few months, Al didn't talk much to Vincent. They both did their jobs, and both seemed content to avoid unnecessary conversations. Mostly they talked about who to lay off next. Then one day, Vincent told Al he would have to take a pay cut. The next month Al and Donna were late with their mortgage payment for the first time. In the months that followed, they were later and later, until they couldn't pay the mortgage at all. They put their house on the market, but in the midst of the recession, there were no buyers. The company shrank to less than half its former size. Al's salary went down to one-third of its highest level. Donna raised some money by holding lawn sales. She sold everything they absolutely didn't need, including their living room furniture.

Al was looking for another job, but so were about 25 percent of the people in the area. And lots of them were looking full time. Al was still going to work every day. Just before the company went out of business, and just before the bank foreclosed on their mortgage, Donna and Al moved down to Mississippi to live with her parents. I haven't heard from them since. Vincent took some of his reserve funds and bought up local real estate that was going cheap. Last I heard he was still in the real estate business.

Did Vincent ruin Al's life? Or was it Al's own fault for taking Vincent's advice? Is Vincent really an unappreciated guardian angel whose great plans for his subordinate were ruined by a recession? If it hadn't been for the recession, wouldn't Al still be happily working for Vincent? If Vincent had left Al alone to make his own family decisions, wouldn't Al and Donna still be living in their nice little house that they enjoyed so much? I don't know the answers to these questions. What I do know is that it was Al and his family who suffered. Ultimately, Al needed to take responsibility for his own life . . . as you need to do for yours.

HOW TO HANDLE
PATERNALISTIC MANAGEMENT

Concentrate on the work. If the boss strays off the subject of work too often, redirect the conversation back to work issues. It can help enormously to go to meetings with written agendas. That way when the boss goes off the subject, you can direct him to the proper agenda item.

Learn how to disagree with the boss without spoiling the friendliness of your relationship. Be supportive; let the boss see you can appreciate her point of view, but then say you see things differently. If your boss is only friendly to you when you agree with her, then she isn't really friendly.

Resist becoming too dependent. If you have allowed yourself to become overly reliant and the boss has gotten used to making your decisions for you, begin to assert your independence. Go slowly at first, but start making your own choices. Let the boss know that you appreciate the help he's given in the past, but then say you think it's now time for you to try out your own wings.

You should realize, of course, that in work-related areas you and the boss may have difficulty differentiating who should be responsible for what. You may be overstepping the legitimate bounds of your job. On the other hand, your boss may feel he has to make all the decisions. The best way to handle such conflicts is to bring them out in the open. Just say, "I would like to take over these responsibilities myself. I need to talk to you about how you see us working together, who should be making which decisions, and how I can become less dependent on you." This, as I have said, relates to work decisions. Choices about your personal life are always exclusively yours to make.

Watch your friendship level. It's nice to say you have a friendly relationship with your boss, but it's rare that a boss and a subordinate can be close friends. You may find it best, without being secretive or suspicious, to keep a comfortable distance between you and the boss.

If your boss plays the social director who insists on getting people involved in out-of-work activities, you may find it hard to take. Evaluate the alternatives. If the job is a good one and the boss is otherwise a competent manager, it may be worth your while to join the softball team to stay on his good side.

12

THE BOSS'S BOSS

THE ROLE OF TOP MANAGEMENT

He could write notes from
Sinai or Olympus; he could
remain unapproachable . . .

John Maynard Keynes
Economic Consequences
of the Peace

Unless you work for the CEO or the owner of a small business, your boss also has a boss, who may or may not be a jerk, a tyrant, a wimp, or a snake. (To keep things straight, I'm going to call your boss's boss "the big boss" and all of the people in the chain of command above your boss "top management.") The big boss will have a profound effect on the way your boss manages you. Your boss will respond to his demands. He will be influenced by the big boss's management style. If he works for a bully, he may conclude that bullying is what the company wants him to do. Jerks lurking in top management can and often do spoil the management style of the entire organization.

Companies develop personalities and cultures because of the influence of one manager on another. This can produce wonderful effects if the top managers instill useful management philosophy in their subordinates. In the case of Felicity Hotels, a small hotel chain, the opposite occurred. Richard Ehrman was the company CEO. Unfortunately, he was also the company SOB. Everyone in the organization felt the sting of his autocratic ways. He used all the cruel tactics of management by fear to keep his people scrambling. He called up the hotels, pretending he was an irate customer. He would needle the person who answered the phone and try to make him lose his temper. If Ehrman succeeded in making the hotel clerk fight back, he fired the clerk on the spot. He insulted the people who reported to him, wilted them with his sarcasm or froze them with his silence. Soon managers who valued their own self-esteem left the company. Those who stayed either already followed Ehrman's style or soon adopted it. Lower level supervisors who stuck around lived in fear. They, too, employed management by intimidation either because they thought it would get them ahead or because bullying others helped them feel less victimized themselves. Because terror tactics work in the short term, the company did well for a few years. Eventually, when just about every manager in the place was a clone of Ehrman, performance took a nosedive. Fortunately the company was bought by a larger chain before it went down one of its many drains. It took the new parent company years to turn around the management style.

Although it is not always as dramatic as it was at Felicity Hotels, it often happens this way. In small, close-knit companies management style can become quite homogeneous.

This is not to say that bosses cannot determine their own management styles. Especially in larger corporations or where groups are geographically removed from the head office, bosses have a great deal of leeway. In such cases, they can often insulate their people from the heat generated by top management.

Besides, all bosses are, at least chronologically, adults. They are responsible for their own actions. We can understand the pressure they might feel from their bosses, but we should not automatically forgive them their foibles and blame the big boss for what they do. Each manager has to be judged by her own actions.

Some of us see the big boss as a demon. Others cast him in the role of avenging angel. Instead of saddling top management with the blame for the boss's bad behavior, we want them to be all-knowing fathers and mothers who can rescue us from the evil monster who is making our work days miserable. We expect them to know what a jerk the boss is and relieve him of his duties. Don't count on it.

TOP MANAGEMENT MAY NOT EVEN KNOW

Top management is unlikely to notice your plight and remove your unbearable boss mainly because they may not know much about your boss's day-to-day activities. Often, managers are not even nearby to see what's going on. In terms of style, bad managers often show a completely different face to the big boss than they do to their employees. Rudy Knox, for instance, runs the packaging area for a record company. The workers in his department have no idea what a Jekyll and Hyde he is. Around them he is a B-movie tough guy. He threatens and belittles them. He seems to have discovered each person's most vulnerable point and pokes it whenever he gets a chance. He teases one about her weight, another about her husband's fidelity, another about the fact that he never went to college.

But this despicable man changes into a fawning, obsequious servant in the presence of the plant manager. Since the plant manager never goes to the packaging department and the packaging workers, almost by definition, never "walk on the carpets," as they say, neither his workers nor his manager ever sees more than one side of Rudy. His peers know what a two-faced person he is, but they figure it's none of their business. They don't interfere.

Like Rudy's boss, your top management may never show up on the scene. They may consider themselves too busy with their "own work." As far as I'm concerned, though, whatever they are doing managers are not doing their jobs if they are unaware of morale problems within their own departments. Unfortunately, that's not the way many top managers see it. They are distracted. They content themselves with superficial knowledge. One study showed that the average senior manager typically spent nine minutes on each topic he dealt with during a business day. What can you learn in nine minutes? Certainly not much, especially about a topic as complex as the motivations and satisfactions of the people who report to the people who report to you. The recent popularity of one minute so-called management all but sanctifies slapdash supervision. Your boss's boss undoubtedly thinks he's doing his job. He may not be.

THEY MAY RECOGNIZE
THE PROBLEM BUT
WILL THEY SOLVE IT?

Then again, the big boss may be well aware of your manager's shortcomings. She may share your opinion of your boss. She may be on the verge of making just the change you have been wishing for. In such a case, your behavior during your current difficulties will be crucial to your future. Suppose the big boss is watching the situation closely, wondering who to promote once she fires your boss. If that's the case, your levelheaded response could mean a big step forward for you. At least, if you behave well, you will not be guilty by association and tossed out with the boss you despise.

Too often, top management knows that a manager has serious shortcomings and leaves him in the job anyway. There are many reasons bad bosses escape the ax. They are expert in some function and therefore considered technically indispensable. They know where the bodies are buried and top management is afraid to incur their wrath by firing or even demoting them. Or it may be that the big boss is a coward. Firing someone is a painful process; he may not have the guts to do it. In Penny Korman's case, it was a hidden loyalty that saved her incompetent boss. Penny worked for Marc Densen, the vice president of production for a toothbrush company. She was the head of cost analysis. She was astute and superb at finding ways to cut the costs of production, a major way to increase profits in many manufacturing operations. But she often had trouble with Marc. He was incapable of understanding or unwilling to listen to many of her ideas. He didn't really stand in her way, but he didn't help her, either. The president, Marc's boss, always appreciated her ideas and respected her ability. But working for Marc frustrated her because she considered him useless.

After a while, she began to ignore Marc altogether and acted as if she reported directly to the president. No one, not Marc and especially not the president, seemed to mind. And Penny could have gone on that way for years, scoring points with the president, being well-rewarded financially and gaining high status and respect in the company, if only she hadn't decided to push Marc out altogether. Her logic at the time was impeccable. *Marc is a cipher, she thought. The president knows that I am doing most of Marc's job. He doesn't even pretend anymore that Marc has a say in what I do. All I have to do is confront the issue. Tell the president he has to get rid of Marc.*

And that's exactly what she did. She picked just the right time, when she had particularly good results to report to the president. In fact, he had just told her what a wonderful contributor she was, how the company profited from her dedication, and how he personally appreciated her efforts. "I'm glad you said that," she said. "It gives me the courage to bring up something that has been bothering me for some time. It's Marc. He contributes nothing to what we're doing here. He's such a hunk of deadwood. Why do you keep him here?"

The president never really answered Penny's question. He made some vague statement about corporate considerations. He didn't embarrass her or himself. He just brought the meeting to a swift end. It was the last really cordial meeting they ever had. After that Penny did her job. He did his. They were civil to one another, but there was none of the joy in working together that there had been. Penny figured the president was a coward, afraid to take the difficult steps necessary to get rid of Marc.

Several years later, when the president retired, so did Marc. After the big retirement party, Penny mentioned to a colleague her curiosity about Marc. "I have never understood why he was protected for all these years. He outlived his usefulness long ago."

"Didn't you know?" Penny's colleague was surprised. "Marc was the president's college roommate. They've been friends for almost fifty years."

Over the years I've heard maybe a hundred excuses. His father and the chairman's father were in the war together. His mother is one of our major stockholders. Her uncle is the department head's golf partner. Incompetence has many defenses. Watch who you criticize; you could paint yourself into a corner politically. Annoying, frustrating, and unfair as it may be, we all have to live with cronyism. It won't go away in your lifetime.

The best approach is the one Penny should have taken. If she was frustrated, she should have asked for more for herself, not less for someone else.

TOP MANAGEMENT
AS OGRE

Sometimes the big boss can wind up taking the rap for something that he is totally unaware of. If your boss is a weakling, he may not have the courage to accept responsibility for his own actions. In such a case, he may tell you that he tried to get you a raise, but that the big boss turned you down. Blaming top management is a favorite dodge of bosses who are trying to avoid resistance from their employees. It's okay once in while, but if your boss uses it constantly, don't buy it.

First of all, not every boss who says, "The old man said no" is sincere. Sometimes bosses never ask at all; sometimes they make only a halfhearted attempt to get agreement. Sometimes they really want to say no in the first place but don't have the nerve. So they present the employee's case but recommend against it. Then they tell the employee top management said no.

If your boss really believes you should get the raise (or promotion or whatever), he must be willing to go to bat for you with his manager. He should fight hard to get you what you deserve. If, time after time, the best he can do is report failure, you should be suspicious. He is either admitting to you that he is ineffectual or that his boss is unreasonable. Either way you are going to have trouble getting what you deserve. You may have a terminal jerk somewhere in the chain of command above you.

If your boss makes her boss out to be an ogre, that's bad. If you create the monster image yourself, you will always have a convenient rationalization for your own failure. You can end up defeating yourself. Here's how Robert Kuhn did just that. When I met him, Robert was already convinced that he and his boss were both victims of the division head. Robert worked as an engineer for an airplane engine manufacturer. He came to me during a training program to ask my advice. He was very vague and secretive. When I finally got it out of him, his concern was faulty specifications on work they were doing for the government. "I can't help it," he told me. "I keep thinking that someday my kid brother will be flying in one of these planes and the engine will fail and he'll die. It's a ridiculous idea, since my brother has no intention of joining the Air Force. But somebody ought to do something."

I agreed with him. "You know the facts," I told him. "You are the logical person to rectify the situation. Have you talked to your boss?"

He told me he had, but that his boss called him a nervous Nellie and said his specifications were overkill on the side of safety. His boss said engines would function very well if the company shaved a little off the specs and made a little better profit.

"He can't believe that," Robert told me. "He's an engineer. He went to MIT, for heaven's sake.

It's his boss who's making him change the specs to increase profits. No self-respecting engineer would make such a decision unless he was pressured into it from above."

I did everything I could to convince Robert that he should go to his boss and make a formal complaint about what he considered a dangerous practice. No matter what I said he just insisted that the division head, not his manager, was not at fault. When I suggested that he go directly to his boss's boss he looked at me in total frustration. "Haven't you been listening," he said. "He's the problem. He's the one who is insisting on making these changes. If I go to him, he'll just throw me out of my job."

I respected Robert's opinion of what was going on in his company. He certainly knew more about it than I did. But all of his theories about who was responsible were based on conjecture. Neither his boss, nor his boss's boss, had ever said anything directly. In the end, it looked as if Robert had created that ogre image for the division head to excuse himself from doing something he was intensely afraid to do—confront the problem.

TOP MANAGEMENT
AS SAVIOR

If you trust your boss's boss you may use her to backstop your boss on problems. If your boss isn't doing his job, you will, as I have advised many times over, go to the boss and talk about the issue and try to resolve it. Make your first requests directly to your boss. But if that fails and your problem is a serious one, you may want to go to his boss to see if you can get satisfaction.

Should you tell your boss that you are going to upper management? The open, honest thing would be to let him know. If you think you can do that without having him try to blockade you, by all means go ahead and let him know what you are doing. If, however, you think your boss will interpret what you are about to do as treasonous, say nothing. Instinct should serve you best here. Whatever you decide, tell the big boss whether or not you have informed your boss of the meeting.

PLAN YOUR
APPEAL TO
UPPER MANAGEMENT

First, decide on your objective and keep it firmly in mind. Pick a positive goal. Avoid objectives like the removal of your boss from his job. Don't hope for his public disgrace. Put out of your mind any thoughts of revenge. If you are going to upper management for retribution, do yourself a favor and go to the nearest employment office instead. What you want is a change in your boss's behavior. Or at the very least, you want management to know that you are not receiving the treatment a loyal, hardworking employee deserves.

An ancillary objective should be to make the best possible impression that you are a rational person with a legitimate gripe who can handle himself in a tight spot. Control your urge to fight loud, confrontational battles. For example, if your boss turns down your brilliant idea for improved procedures, you can go to the big boss and shout, "If this company really wants us to be more efficient, how come they keep idiots like Bernard on the job?" Or you can wait until your anger abates and present your idea coherently and persuasively to top management. If you preserve your reputation and your working relationship with all levels of management, you'll have a better chance of selling your idea.

Plan your communications according to the advice in Chapter four. Lay out your recommendation, have the facts to back it up, be specific and BRIEF. Talk about the future, not the past. Talk about behavior, not about personality. You know the drill by now. Above all, go in with a picture of a positive outcome firmly in mind.

Reserve trips over your boss's head for serious problems. Remember the tales of your childhood. Chicken Little Meets the Boy Who Cried Wolf is no script for a lifetime.

If you have a serious problem with the way things are managed in your organization and you feel there is no one in authority to whom you can turn, write your resume and start reading the want ads. Move before your motivation dies. If you can't find one person in authority whom you can trust, either the company is completely wrong for you or you are working for a jerk organization. That, as you are about to discover, can be hazardous to your health.

13

WORKING FOR A JERK CORPORATION

There had been absolutely nobody at the top who had understood how things really worked, what it was all about, what was really going on.

Kurt Vonnegut
Galápagos

had a story to tell you to open this chapter, but I've decided to save it until later. You see, while I was working on this book, I woke up one morning to hear a tragic, moving report that, I am sad to say, dramatically illustrates my point. I was listening to "Morning Edition" on National Public Radio. The date was February 20, 1986. Here is the content of that broadcast:

The report concerned the Rogers Commission's investigation of the effects of cold weather on the *Challenger* explosion. According to the head of the panel, William Rogers, three top NASA officials had not heard that Morton Thiokol engineers had raised serious concerns the day before the space shuttle disaster. Thiokol built the *Challenger*'s solid rocket boosters.

This introduction was followed by two on-site reports. The first was from Huntsville, Alabama, where a reporter described a Morton Thiokol engineer, his eyes red with tears. "I fought like hell to stop that launch," the engineer said. "I'm so torn up inside I can hardly talk about it, even now." The engineers had described to the reporter what happened the day before the launch. NASA and Thiokol management refused to talk about it.

The day before the disaster at about noon at Thiokol headquarters in Brigham City, Utah, several key engineers learned of the unusually low temperatures around the shuttle launch pad in Cape Canaveral. It was, they realized, colder than it had ever been just before a launch. The engineers hurried to speak to one another in company hallways. They all agreed it was urgent that they warn top management. The shuttle could be in serious trouble.

Worried engineers crowded around the desk of Thiokol vice president Robert Lund and showed him the evidence. If temperatures in Florida stayed as low as they had been, they said, the seals holding the rocket together might fail during takeoff. One engineer said, "We all knew if the seals failed the shuttle would blow up."

At six P.M. the same evening, a more formal meeting took place in Thiokol's main conference room. Several engineers and four top managers studied charts and photographs of rocket seals. They agreed that, given their test results, it was too risky to allow the shuttle launch.

At eight P.M., they made a conference call to NASA. One by one, four engineers presented the troubling facts. Bob Lund ended their presentation to NASA with Thiokol's official recommendation: Do not launch the shuttle tomorrow.

The NASA officials were shocked. George Hardy of NASA's Marshall Space Flight Center in Huntsville said, "I am appalled by your recommendation." Another NASA executive, Larry Mulloy, said Thiokol didn't have enough proof that the cold weather would cause the seals to fail. The engineers vehemently disagreed; some almost shouted with anger. They insisted that the launch should be postponed until the temperature climbed above fifty. And at that point, one engineer reported, Larry Mulloy exclaimed "My God, Thiokol, when do you want me to launch, next April?"

At 8:30, Thiokol managers put NASA on hold and asked their engineers if they were sure. "Absolutely," they replied, and virtually no one disagreed. But now Thiokol's general manager Jerry Mason said, "Look, this has got to be a management decision." With a dozen engineers looking on in frustration and anger, he asked the other three managers to decide. They each gave the nod to go ahead with the launch.

One engineer said he didn't know why the managers overruled them. "As you know our company's competing with several other corporations to get future shuttle contracts. I can only guess," the engineer said, "at the enormous pressures they were feeling."

At 8:45 P.M., Thiokol General Manager Mason got back on the line with NASA and told them, "Okay we'll approve the launch after all."

NASA's Mulloy asked the Thiokol managers to "sign the document right away and send it to us by telefax."

Only one top Thiokol manager, Alan McDonald, refused to sign the paper. After the meeting broke up, the engineers went home feeling downtrodden and defeated. And they were scared. "I kept having fantasies that night," said one engineer, "that at the moment of ignition the shuttle would blow up instantly. See, we thought that if the seals failed the shuttle would never get off the pad. There'd just be a big fireball and everything would vanish. I was so scared I didn't even want to watch the launch."

The next morning, that engineer along with fifty other collegues, watched the launch in the same conference room where they'd met the previous night. "When the shuttle lifted off the pad," he said, "I thought, gee, it's going all right. It's a piece of cake. And when we were one minute into the launch a friend turned to me and he said 'Oh God, we made it, we made it.' Then a few seconds later the shuttle blew up and we all knew exactly what happened."

Another reporter filed a story from Brigham City, Utah. He told the story of a Morton Thiokol engineer who prayed as he watched *Challenger* lift off. The reporter couldn't tell the engineer's name or his job title because he felt his job depended on secrecy. What he did tell about was that engineer's feelings.

On January 28, the engineer prayed a divine act would guide the shuttle safely into space. He feared the seals in the solid rocket boosters would fail in the chilly morning air and cause disaster. As the shuttle lifted off and *Challenger* seemed okay, he changed to a prayer of thanks. Then, *Challenger* exploded. The engineer sat quietly and cried.

Three weeks later, he was haunted by the disaster. Although he and his colleagues had tried to prevent the launch, he regretted that he had not done more. He said NASA, which had always put safety first, "had a brain spasm." "They forgot their code of conduct," he said. He regretted that when Lawrence Mulloy of NASA asked 'My God, Thiokol, when do you want me to launch, next April?' that he didn't stand up and say, "If that's when it's warm, yes." But he didn't.

This once-proud space program engineer talked of his depression, of meeting with psychiatric specialists Thiokol would provide. He said he felt NASA managers had coerced his company into approving the launch, but he blamed his fellow Thiokol engineers and himself for not insisting on a postponement. "I should have done more," he said, "I could have done more."

People dying before the eyes of an entire nation—private grief of frustrated people who tried and failed to prevent the catastrophe. These are our equivalent of Greek tragedy, incalculably more grievous than the ancient plays because the people who died and the people who mourn are real. And the tragic flaw is not in one person but imbedded in the very nature of our institutions. In a separate report in the *New York Times*, a space agency analyst is quoted as saying that NASA had a "gung-ho, can-do" atmosphere that made it difficult to raise concerns about safety. You can't send people into space without the gung-ho attitude, but that outlook also harbored the seeds of the project's destruction.

The Rogers Commission that investigated the shuttle accident concluded that it was indeed the faulty seals that caused the disaster. It recommended a redesign of the seals and of NASA's management. The former will be a lot easier than the latter. How will they change the way people work together in groups? Our organizations make it nearly impossible for unpopular information to be communicated, much less acted upon. This is the weakness that must be removed, but it will not go easily.

If you don't believe me, think about this: In preparing its report, the Rogers Commission had internal battles about one section which, supposedly, was too harsh in its criticism of NASA. Commission-member Dr. Richard Feynman, a 1965 Nobel Prize winner in physics, released his own separate report one day after the commission study. Dr. Feynman's thirteen-page document was much more critical of NASA. Reportedly, the commission and Feynman had different ideas on how strongly and clearly the commission's findings should be stated. Feynman's language was evidently too blunt for the body of the commission's report. It got relegated to a delayed appendix. In other words, the Rogers Commission seems to have suffered a mild case of the same malady as infected the organization it investigated—when the truth might be unpopular, bury it.

This is the most tragic way that whole organizations can become jerks. There are many others. In almost any industry you will find them. We call our places of business "firms," but some are infirm and some are infirmaries. We need to take care before we commit ourselves to the influence of the organization.

As children, we learn from our families the art

of fitting in, of belonging to a group. In every group we join, we will pay the price of membership. To be valued by the other members, we must respect the rules, pay attention to the things the group values, and ignore the things it ignores. We buy the cozy feeling of acceptance by filtering out information the group prefers to deny, by not asking embarrassing questions. Eventually we start to think the way the group thinks.

If this is true—and I'm sure it is—we must be very careful what groups we join. Once we are in them, we will feel the pressure to conform, and we will begin to rationalize the way we think and act. But if we are truly going to help our group succeed, we must also be willing to take the risk of questioning bad assumptions and softheaded opinions. We must have the courage to communicate the information that may save the group from disaster. If we comply until the accident happens or the fiasco is in progress, we may see our own futures go down the tubes.

Now, let's talk about how you can identify a jerk corporation and how you can save yourself if you happen to be working for one.

DANGER SIGNALS
OF CORPORATE MALAISE

The first sign of corporate trouble may be financial problems. Every organization has its financial ups and downs. You should not be alarmed and run for the want ads just because your company has a bad quarter. That would be a major mistake. But if the organization has serious financial difficulties, take a hard look at how your management is dealing with them. They must take the sometimes difficult steps needed to insure the health of the organization. Watch to see if they have the guts to do the right thing.

You may find that the right thing will not necessarily please you personally. Cuts in pay and benefits can result from hard times. If your employer needs to make such cuts to save the organization, they will affect your pocketbook. You may want to think about going to a healthier company. Only you can decide how loyal you want to be. But remember, the worst thing an employer can do to his employees is go out of business. Many people would rather have a job at lower pay or benefits rather than no job at all.

But be suspicious if your company's management asks the employees to bear all the burden of financial troubles—for instance, in one holding company, the top five officers voted themselves each a $25,000 bonus four months before the company went bankrupt. If executives are going to take the money and run when they see the organization heading for trouble, how can I preach loyalty to you?

In fact, be skeptical about any company that forgets about the basics and tries to make its money by financial manipulation. The only healthy ways for an organization to succeed financially are through constant innovation or superior customer satisfaction. If your top management doesn't seem to know this simple rule for running a business, run.

Other obvious danger signals will come from the behavior of the employees. How do they spend their time? How dedicated are they to the organization's goals? I can't tell you how many people I have heard say, "Well, you know this place? It's a zoo." I have almost thirty client companies and none of them runs a zoological park. But employees in many of them speak of their organizations in these terms. Okay, we're always going to have a certain amount of griping from the inmates of any institution; however, if the complaints constitute a major daily activity, we've got trouble.

Watch out for organizational superstitions. All healthy organizations have unwritten rules, ways of doing things that are not part of the procedure but ingrained in the atmosphere and relationships of the people. When these group habits are positive—like always considering the customer reaction or making sure all people affected by a decision have a say in it—they are among an organization's most important strengths. When they are counterproductive—like insisting that everyone put everything in writing or spending a lot of energy on whose office is bigger than whose—they can destroy the organization.

You will find these destructive habits easy to identify; they are the things nobody thinks are smart but everybody does because everyone else is doing them. For instance, at one advertising agency I know, every document that goes to a client begins with the same two words: "This forwards." Letter after letter—"This forwards the agency's recommendation for . . ." or "This forwards the results of the agency's analysis of . . ."

When I first noticed this habit, I called it to the attention of the trainees in my effective writing program. They all agreed that the practice was ludicrous. They knew that stating the purpose of a letter in the first sentence was a fine idea, but they were sure there were other ways to do it. They argued that an advertising agency should show its creativity by thinking of new and different ways to say things—that such repetition communicated to the clients that the agency might be in a rut. No one wanted to start every document with "This forwards," but they all did it because everyone else did. They were afraid to stray from the norm. After five or six years of trying to get them to change it, I gave up.

Everyone in the agency believed that no letter would be approved without the hated beginning. Some people became managers still believing that, so they never let a document leave the agency without those words at the beginning. Soon, we spent a few minutes in each training program discussing the issue. New people expressed their surprise and dismay that what otherwise seemed (at least at first) to be a sensible company would have such a silly requirement. I told them they were right, but the phrase was a corporate superstition. They should fight it only if they thought it was worth it.

When I brought the issue to the attention of one of the agency's top managers, he told me there were no rules about such a thing. But he started his letters with, guess what?—"This forwards." After years of working with the agency, I believe the superstition is just a symptom of a more pervasive disease. The whole place seems to be preoccupied with form and pays too little attention to substance.

That's the problem with this sort of seemingly silly corporate habit. It is hard to imagine any organization completely free of such nonsense. But it is equally difficult to separate harmless groupthink from widespread mass craziness.

You can tell a lot about the severity of an organization's problems by looking at how the people in the company relate to one another. If they are not on speaking terms, or if they are constantly badmouthing one another, they will be unable to cooperate with one another. If they form into cliques or other closed groups, or if they spend their time bickering and waging memo wars, they will interfere with one another. The organization will be inefficient.

People work together in groups for the added power they get or the fun they have. When the output of the group is greater than that which could be produced by the individual efforts of members then we have a worthwhile group effort. This is one of the greatest assets and greatest joys of being a member of the human race. If your work group doesn't produce this synergy, if everyone is doing his own thing, you will not only miss the satisfaction of working with the group, the company will lose its competitive edge.

POP QUIZ:
IS THIS PLACE AS BAD
AS IT FEELS?

Oftentimes, people who are in a bad environment blame themselves when they feel out of place and out of sorts. Before you conclude it is you who is at fault, use these questions to rate your company:

ALWAYS	ALMOST ALWAYS	SOMETIMES	ALMOST NEVER	NEVER	
4	3	2	1	0	1. Is there general agreement in the organization on what its goals are?
4	3	2	1	0	2. Does the organization accomplish these goals?
4	3	2	1	0	3. Does it show a profit?
4	3	2	1	0	4. Is it financially sound?
4	3	2	1	0	5. Does it have sufficient assets to insure long-term continuity?

4 3 2 1 0   6. Are the organization's goods or services of high quality?

4 3 2 1 0   7. Does top management continually work to improve quality?

4 3 2 1 0   8. Does the organization satisfy the needs of all people concerned—its customers?

4 3 2 1 0   9. its employees?

4 3 2 1 0   10. its owners or stockholders?

4 3 2 1 0   11. its suppliers and creditors?

4 3 2 1 0   12. the community and government?

4 3 2 1 0   13. Does the organization respond to change and still maintain its basic character?

4 3 2 1 0   14. Are the employees motivated to give the organization what it needs to succeed?

4 3 2 1 0   15. Do the managers and employees have the expertise to do their jobs well?

4 3 2 1 0   16. Does the company train its people to keep them up to date?

4 3 2 1 0   17. Do employees participate in decisions that affect their work-life?

4 3 2 1 0   18. Do the best people stay with the organization?

4 3 2 1 0   19. Is there a general atmosphere of cooperation and satisfaction?

4 3 2 1 0   20. Is bad news allowed to surface and be dealt with?

4 3 2 1 0   21. Does the company have a good safety record?

4 3 2 1 0   22. Do people who work for the company have a clear understanding of what they are supposed to be doing?

4 3 2 1 0   23. Is there a consistent system of job titles and salaries for all positions?

4 3 2 1 0   24. Does the company promote from within?

4 3 2 1 0   25. Are there regular performance evaluations with opportunities for employee comment?

4 3 2 1 0   26. Are the benefits your company provides comparable to those available from other companies in the industry or in the area?

4 3 2 1 0   27. Do your skills and talents match what the company wants and needs?

4 3 2 1 0   28. Can you successfully compete for better jobs you might want?

4 3 2 1 0   29. Do the products or services of the company interest you?

4 3 2 1 0   30. Does your personality fit well with the character of the company?

Add up your company's score. Here are some general conclusions you can draw; read them but don't hand in your resignation until you read what comes next:

120—91 You may want to stay until retirement.

90—51 Get all the satisfaction and training you can. Work to improve the weak or missing elements. You and your colleagues may be able to turn the organization into a real winner.

50—26 Start looking for a better place. The organization probably doesn't deserve a person with your talent and intelligence.

25—0 Write your resume. Call a headhunter. Or vegetate until early retirement.

Caveat: These are a powerful lot of questions. They define all of the criteria you need to judge whether or not you are working for a healthy organization that can satisfy your needs. The problem is that some of the issues raised in the quiz may seem unimportant to you. If so, you should ignore them. That makes it difficult to use the rating scale at the end of this quiz to make a general conclusion about the company. For instance, if you rate the company a "4" on everything but it consistently fails to make a profit, you don't have any future there no matter how comfortable it feels.

SHOULD YOU JUST LEAVE?

If you want to know whether you should resign from an organization, watch who else is leaving. If the people you admire most are walking out, consider leaving, too. A number of people at Jackson & Chester found this out the hard way. They should have taken a clue from what happened to Denny Fisher, the most popular manager at the company. Denny had a reputation for supporting his people and for training them very well. Even people who didn't work directly for him admired his style.

Jackson & Chester is a holding company that owned and operated computer stores in eight major southern cities. Things had gone along swimmingly at the headquarters for several years. The company grew and so did the head office staff.

Then, Mssrs. Jackson and Chester, who started the first store ten years ago, decided to sell out. Everyone thought it was a good sign. Like many entrepreneurs, they were brilliant about starting a business but not good at ongoing administration. They were difficult managers—too demanding of their employees. The employees expected the new management to be easier to get along with.

When the owners decided to go on to other things, they went public with the company, but they maintained a controlling interest. They appointed David Jarvis to be the president. This is just what everyone expected. But no one was sure what it meant. Jarvis had some marketing brilliance. That was to the good, but once in a while he showed some ruthlessness with people. The employees watched and waited. It didn't take long for them to see just what Jarvis had in mind.

Everyone was secretly hoping that Denny would play a major role in the management after Jackson and Chester left. They wanted Denny's management style to influence what happened in the company. It didn't turn out that way. Instead, Jarvis picked Rudy Maddox to be his second in command. As much as everyone liked Denny, they were afraid of Rudy. He was unpredictable and hot-tempered. They couldn't believe Denny was passed over in favor of such a nasty guy. Morale hit the cellar.

Soon afterward, to no one's surprise and everyone's dismay, Denny left to open his own computer store. Many people hoped Denny would take them along, to rescue them from what looked like a bleak future at J & C. Lots of them talked about quitting then, but few did. Later, they were sorry.

They threw Denny a wild farewell party, complete with belly dancers and big band music. After that a pall descended over the organization. With low morale and little respect from their management, many employees began to work halfheartedly. Worse yet, they were afraid to tell Jarvis and Rudy what they thought about anything. Out of fear, they put on an information "freeze," and their managers had to make their decisions in the dark. A loss of business resulted. Eventually the whole organization faltered. People were laid off in droves. Many of them said the same thing. "I should have seen the handwriting on the wall when Denny left."

If everyone who cares leaves the organization, the company will lose its viability. In some cases all the competent people go, and you wind up with nothing but deadwood. Every organization has a few people who have outstayed their usefulness, but if you look around and see a lumberyard, you may be looking at an organization about to go under.

Commonly, organizations get into trouble by going to extremes. Every group has a set of traditions and definitions for appropriate behavior. If the company has too many unwritten rules, it becomes tradition bound. "How" becomes more important than "what." People look not at the content of presentations, for instance, but at how they are structured. Even trite and superficial analysis will be accepted and praised if it is presented with enough panache. Brilliant insights will be rejected if the person presenting them doesn't use enough color slides.

The opposite extreme is also common—many organizations change constantly. The top management can't make up its mind about what it wants the company to be. They latch onto the latest fad management technique and use it until another fad appears. The direction of the company changes more often than hemline fashions. I once worked with a company run by an executive committee that couldn't agree on anything. The only consensus they could reach was to hire consultants to help them decide what to do about the future of the company. They hired a series of consulting firms and went through a series of reorganizations, centralizing and decentralizing different aspects of the company's work. The employees were in a constant state of upheaval. Profitability suffered. But top management felt safe because they were taking the advice of top-notch, very expensive, and famous management consultants. How could they go wrong?

We have already spoken in Chapter Six about the moral and social problems caused by unethical managers. Sometimes group-think causes whole organizations to lose sight of honesty and what is right. A company can go over the cliff. The A.H. Robbins Company finally filed for bankruptcy after thousands of lawsuits were filed against it by people who had been injured by its product, the Dalkon Shield intrauterine device. In *At Any Cost*, a book documenting what happened at Robbins, Morton Mintz recounted the story of one employee who saw that the shield design could promote the growth of bacteria but who also worked out a simple solution to the problem. But instead of admitting the difficulty, implementing the employee's suggestion, and trying to cut its losses, the company's management ignored him, reprimanded him, and forced him out of his job. Company executives misled doctors and government officials and destroyed incriminating documents. People were injured and employees lost their jobs.

How can groups of people bring themselves to make such decisions? How can they not see that the profits and reputations they hope to protect will only be destroyed by such duplicity? Self-deception seems to cause people to hear and see only that which fits their preconceived notions and inner desires. Somehow, employees support the efforts of the group, even if those efforts are ultimately destructive. If your company's management imitates the famous trio of monkeys, you and all of your colleagues are in for trouble.

EFFECTS OF
CORPORATE JERKDOM

Job insecurity is the major difficulty when working for a badly managed company. Mel Peabody found that out. He expected to stay with the power company for his entire career. He went there right out of high school, worked hard, and trusted that the people who ran the company knew what they were doing.

When the executives decided to build a nuclear plant in a highly populated area, they were immediately opposed by citizens and environmental groups. They ignored the objections of the community and went ahead, a decision which drove the company to economic chaos. Years later they had spent $4.1 billion (fifteen times the original budget) and the plant hadn't produced watt one. They instituted pay cuts for managers and a 20 percent staff cut among what the newspapers called "lower level" employees. Mel was one of the people who lost his job. After thirty-six years with the company, he was out. He had a daughter in medical school and a son in college. At the age of fifty-three, he is a vigorous man who, according to the government's life expectancy tables, has another twenty-four years of life to live. But he's not sure that, at his age, he'll ever get another job.

Hundreds of Mel's coworkers, many of whom had been with the company for more than twenty-five years, went in the same purge. There is nothing they could have done to compensate for the bad decisions made in the boardroom.

Not all of the problems caused by poor leadership result in layoffs, but poor management stunts corporate growth and eats up corporate profitability. It results in a dearth of promotion opportunities and strings of low, if any, raises.

There is also considerable frustration. In overly rigid corporate environments, you will find yourself mired in red tape and stressed by having to adhere to useless rules. You will feel that you are just a number. Decisions will be delayed, and your efforts will be wasted. You can feel no one cares about what you are doing. Your creativity will be stifled.

If you go to work every day and face that kind of atmosphere, you will have to drag yourself to work. If all of your coworkers are equally demoralized, you will find life at work a dehumanizing experience. You and your colleagues will become alienated and apathetic. In such grim circumstances, your entire existence can be diminished. How then can you produce results that will lead to real group success?

If the organization is in a constant state of flux, you will find it difficult to feel secure enough to concentrate on what you are doing. You will be frustrated because your work is not linked to any real objective. You may be faced with exorbitant requirements, confusing directions, and unreasonable deadlines.

If the company makes a practice of cutting corners, if you daily face the unethical behavior of others, your own self-esteem will be eroded. If you see people whose methods you despise being rewarded, you may have to pay for your tolerance of such villainy with the lining of your stomach.

YOU MAY JUST
BE OUT OF SYNC

You may find that your organization suffers from none of these definable ills, yet you still feel uncomfortable and out of sorts. It may just be that you and the entire company are having a personality conflict. Especially if you have worked in only one or two places, you may not realize that organizations have distinct characters.

As I travel from company to company, I often feel like an anthropologist visiting tribes. I see real differences in the way people relate to one another, sometimes even in different locations of the same company. Groups are friendly or brusque, cutthroat or supportive. If the prevailing culture of your organization doesn't match your own personality, you will feel uncomfortable no matter how hard you try.

In fact, some analysts feel you can even characterize whole industries. In grossly simplified form, here are some descriptions of personalities that go with certain industries:

Orderly, punctual people who are detail-oriented and cautious will fit in well in heavily regulated industries like insurance companies, banks, pharmaceutical companies, utilities, and government agencies.

People who are willing to take risks and wait a long time to see if they pan out are best suited for new, capital-intensive ventures, oil companies, and investment banks.

Risk-oriented people who like to see themselves as glamorous or aggressive but who need immediate feedback on how they're doing make out best in advertising, the entertainment business, consulting, venture capital, publishing, and the fashion industry. They also are drawn to medicine and police work.

Energetic, friendly people who don't like risks but who don't mind if they have to keep going despite setbacks make out well in sales and marketing-oriented companies.

There is, of course, no way we can reduce such a complex subject to four simple paragraphs, but I hope these brief descriptions help you understand what things to consider when you analyze whether you are in the right industry for you.

When your personality matches the character of the organization, you will instinctively make many right decisions and you will feel comfortable and important to the organization. You will also find friends as well as teammates among your co-workers. Where your disposition is at odds with the corporate personality, you will feel out of sorts, be zigging when everyone else is zagging. You will wonder how the people around you can stand the place, much less enjoy it as much as they do.

One excellent measure of your compatibility with a company is your feeling about the product or service it provides. If the central work of the organization interests you, you will respond enthusiastically to your role in it. For example, I'm sure I would enjoy working in almost any capacity for an opera company. I love the art form that much. If you are a computer specialist who is fascinated with clothing, you will be happier if plying your computer trade in a clothing company. On the other hand, if you don't care anything about the stock market, brokerage firm work will scarcely inspire you regardless of how removed your job is from actual stock trading.

HOW TO COPE WITH A JERK CORPORATION

If you feel out of step or that the organization is beyond redemption, ask yourself why you still work there. It may be that you have a hard time separating yourself from anything. Just knowing that leave-taking always makes you uncomfortable may help you extricate yourself. For instance, my friend Nicoletta understands that she hates going through any change. She accommodates herself and makes little improvements to keep a bad situation tolerable. She worked for nearly two years for a boss who piled on the work and never showed any appreciation. Whenever she became overwhelmed or disgusted she would go to the boss and complain. He would lighten her load or tell her how much he appreciated her. She would feel better and her boss's behavior would improve for a few days. But soon she was back to her old level of dissatisfaction. Finally, she realized that things would have to get worse before they got better. So she stopped asking the boss to improve matters. She let herself become more and more disgusted until the pain of staying outweighed the pain of leaving. Then she left.

You may be staying in an unsatisfying job because you feel a certain loyalty to your friends in the organization or because you hesitate to leave them behind. You may stay to avoid breaking your ties with the people you like. Remember that you don't have to end your friendship with them because you don't see them at work every day.

It's also worth considering this: If you let your friends "keep" you in a place that is ultimately wrong for you, you may end up resenting them. Then you will grow to dislike them anyway. I worked with one person who was close to a number of our coworkers. But then there came a time when he really needed to leave. His job was a dead end, and he was frustrated, but he couldn't tear himself away. Finally, he quarreled with his best friends. Then he left. I think unconsciously he had to reject his friends to allow himself to go on to better things. What a pity he couldn't tear himself away gracefully.

IF YOU STAY

If you decide to remain in the organization even though you are aware of its faults, you must have some hope that the place can be salvaged. Do what you can to change the way things are done. Narrow your goals for the time being, pick a few issues you want to challenge, and give them your best.

Get as much satisfaction as you can out of doing your own job well. Find the other competent people in the organization. If the company hasn't gone belly up, there must be a few people who know what to do and are doing it. Work with them. Exchange favors with them. Form a support group; enlist their help to try to change the most destructive corporate habits.

Learn to play the game, to look as if you are complying with the silly rules. For example, if you work in a place that puts a premium on being busy and you actually don't have enough to do, learn to look fully employed. Am I telling you to be dishonest, to lie? I hope not. But if it doesn't hurt your conscience, go along with what the others expect. If staying means transgressing against important values, don't do it.

IF YOU DECIDE TO LEAVE

Avoid similar traps. Before you take another job, ask some questions to make sure the company is worthy of you. Most people go to job interviews worried about whether they will be accepted. Go to make a good impression, of course, but go primarily to find out about the company. What does it do to show it appreciates its employees? How does the top management insure the financial security of the company? How would you characterize the personality of this organization? You can't ask all the questions in one interview, but pick two or three that are most important. Before you sign on, find out if the company is on the right track for you.

14

IF ALL
BOSSES
SEEM BAD

*And art made tongue-tied
by authority*

William Shakespeare
Sonnet 66

John Carr simply could not keep a job. He quarreled with every boss he ever had. He said they were all stupid. Sometimes he lasted a few months, sometimes only a few days. Usually, though, sooner than later, he either quit or got fired. His wife was the main wage earner in the family. In the beginning when he lost a job, she commiserated with him. She knew that some bosses were difficult, and that John was a proud person who wouldn't want to be pushed around. But as a result of John's constant job hopping, he and his family moved nineteen times in twelve years; his children went to eleven different grammar schools. Over the years, when John came home with complaints about his boss, his wife found it harder and harder to believe that John was right and yet another manager was totally at fault, idiotic, and incompetent. After years of constant change and financial problems, she eventually lost all her sympathy for her husband.

Finally, when the children were in high school, John's long-suffering wife couldn't take it any more. She left him and was finally able to give her children some stability.

John's case is extreme. But many people have difficulty with authority. They don't like anyone to have power over them. The very nature of the boss-subordinate relationship rubs them the wrong way. Let's examine briefly that relationship and see how it might relate to you.

Bosses have authority over their employees. When we say "authority" in this context we mean they have the right to make decisions about what the employee does, how he does it, how much of it he is required to do, etc. To exercise that right the boss must have some power. By power, we mean the boss can, to a certain extent, control the actions of the employee. That power can come from several sources.

It can be organizational. The company puts a manager in charge of a work unit and says, in effect, this whole organization will abide by the decisions you make regarding the work of that group. The extreme of this would be a military unit during combat, where traditionally the commanding officer has the right to take the life of any soldier who will not follow orders. (Imagine John Carr under those circumstances.)

Most modern corporations actually give very little authority to their managers, especially supervisors at lower levels. In fact, in many cases bosses have responsibilities without having the commensurate authority to carry them out. For instance, it is unusual these days to find a manager who has the sole right to hire and fire employees. And raises, as we have discussed, are decided through elaborate systems and procedures. If you think about it, most corporate employees are immune from bosses taking precipitous actions against them.

Most bosses' real power comes from their ability to control company resources. They get to decide who gets which projects, who gets to work with which group. And although they usually cannot make decisions unilaterally, they can influence important ones concerning pay and promotions.

It is this power of opinion that is strongest in modern bosses. They have the right to judge our work. Frequently they also pass judgment on our characters or personalities. To the extent that their opinions are respected by others in the company, bosses can have a great deal to say about our futures. But we give them that power first by taking the job and second by wanting the pay raises and promotions the company has to offer.

Perhaps the strongest personal power of opinion comes from our need for the boss's approval. If you need a person's admiration, that person has a great deal of control over you. In this case, the subordinate invests the boss with power by needing her regard.

There's a paradox here. Some people empower their bosses by deciding to work for them or by needing their approval and then resent the bosses' authority. They repeat this process with every boss they ever have.

Now think about yourself. If your current boss is intolerable, you have my sympathy. But how many bosses in the past have had the same flaws as this one has? If you are going through a long string of bad bosses, the problem may be more in you than in them.

ANALYZING PROBLEMS
WITH AUTHORITY

Some people get into trouble with bosses and other authority figures because they have unrealistic expectations of what and who the boss is. They expect the boss to be a perfect parent who with flawless methods, absolute kindness, and infallible judgment solves all problems, dispels all insecurities, and makes the employee a happy person. They expect to agree with every decision the boss makes. Usually people who suffer from these false hopes don't even realize what they are doing. They see their disappointments as individual events, not as a pattern. I was drawn into the same trap in sympathizing with a friend. His name is Phil Gonzalez.

When I met Phil, he had just taken a job coordinating training for a medical supply company. I had worked with his predecessor, who was a cold and rigid person. Phil was a welcome relief—funny, warmhearted, and quirky. I liked him immediately, and we worked happily together from the outset.

Almost immediately, Phil started to ask me questions about his boss, Lou Kirshwin. To tell you the truth, I never liked Lou all that much myself. I vaguely alluded to my lukewarm feelings about Lou. After that, almost every time I met with Phil he recounted some story illustrating what a snake Lou was. They all sounded plausible; they fit in with Lou's personality and the sorts of things I had seen Lou do in the past. I believed Phil. Lou was looking worse and worse to both of us. When Lou was transferred to another division, Phil and I were both glad to see him go. We both thought Phil had a good chance of getting Lou's old job. It didn't happen that way.

Lou's job went to Anita Worth. I didn't know her at all; she was a peer of Phil's, working in another group. Phil said he wasn't that upset, but everything else he said indicated that he was. He told me that he had been in the job longer than Anita, that he had more experience in the field than she did. "But," he said, "everyone in the company knows why she's getting the job. She's sleeping with the president."

Even from a good friend, that remark was more than I could take. "I'm going to give you my usual response to that remark, Phil," I said. "If women could sleep their way to the top, there would be more women at the top."

He insisted that he was right. "Everyone in the company knows about it," he said. Up until then, I had believed everything Phil had told me. Because I like him and because he was such a good, competent, hardworking guy, I believed much of what he told me over the next year. I never totally accepted what he said about Anita. I got to know her in her new capacity, and whatever else she was doing, she was doing a very good job.

But Phil didn't get along with her. He told me she criticized him for things that didn't seem true from my perspective. I figured there was a personality conflict between them. I was glad for him when he got a promotion to another division. I worked with him there, too, and guess what? His new boss was a problem. When I met him, I agreed one hundred percent with Phil. The general manager of the new division was a bully and a liar. I had that on my own observation.

When Phil decided he wanted out, it seemed like a good idea. He had been with the company over five years by then. And one of my other clients had an open spot that looked perfect for Phil. It was a step up from what he was doing and would be a little stretch for him, but he was bright and eager. He could do it. Best of all, he would be working for one of the best managers I knew. There would be no hanky-panky, no capricious and arbitrary decisions in the new job.

I talked to Phil. He pushed hard for the job and got it. We were both very happy that he was making a new start. He was there only a few weeks when the complaints started again. There was a difference. Not only was Phil's new boss at fault. This time Phil blamed me, too. He said I wanted him to fail, that I set him up in that job because I wanted to use him to get me more business with the new company. Now Phil had two ogres to blame: his boss and me. I was shocked at his reaction. He stopped speaking to me.

I heard that he had gotten another new job shortly afterward. Since I no longer see him, I don't know how he's making out. I feel bad. I wonder what the problem is with Phil. His shrink may be able to relate all this back to something that happened in his childhood. I don't know much about psychoanalysis, so I won't guess. What I do know is that Phil won't ever be satisfied with any boss until he changes his way of looking at the boss-subordinate relationship.

We all have this tendency: When things are going well we like to take the credit (we say, "I was lucky; I was smart; I was in the right place at the right time"), but when things are going poorly, we look for somewhere else to put the blame (we say, "They gave me too much to do; he didn't tell me what the priorities were; my boss is a jerk"). Since the boss is ostensibly in charge, it is easy to blame her for any work-related problem. Since we spend so much of our waking life at work, we can more easily blame the boss for our general dissatisfaction with life. As a matter of fact, that may have been part of the problem with Phil. He was single; he put most of his energy and hopes for satisfaction into his work. Maybe he expected the job to compensate him for what he otherwise would have gotten from love and family relationships.

It is also easy to point to the boss's personality as the source of the problem. It's right there, sticking out and visible. We can gloss over subtler problems of trust, or thornier questions of organization, corporate structure, and job design. As long as we have the boss's character as a convenient scapegoat, why bother with the intricacies of complex problem analysis?

For some people, merely knowing that another person has power over them makes them insecure. Understanding that the boss can veto your ideas can frustrate you. Just having a boss means that your options are constrained. That in itself could make you angry. Some people seem to rebel instinctively against authority. Their resentment is out of proportion to what is really going on. The boss is automatically the enemy, an obstacle to be overcome, a hindrance. Authoritarian bosses are unbearable. Even participative, supportive bosses are only tolerable.

This attitude evokes a negative response in the boss. Once the boss senses the employee's hostility, he loses trust. In Phil Gonzalez's story, Anita had evaluated Phil and found him wanting. That shouldn't have surprised me; how could Phil have avoided broadcasting his disdain for her?

Phil was one of the angry ones. Sarah Johnson was just as bad off for being super-compliant. She worked as a secretary for the development group in a toy company. Her assumption was that she was supposed to comply perfectly with whatever her bosses told her to do, regardless of how inane or insane the request. She worked for three designers and an engineer. At first only one of them, a designer named Steve, pushed her around. He had her typing his personal letters, and she was supposed to keep important family dates—like his sister's birthday and his parents' wedding anniversary—in her calendar and remind him of them. This was on top of all the administrative work for the whole group. She hated it. But she swallowed her anger and did what she was told with a smile. To her, being a subordinate meant never talking back, never questioning. She saw herself as having no rights whatsoever.

Pretty soon others in the group, seeing that

she did not object to Steve's requests, asked her to do personal favors for them as well. Soon they were all happy and cozy with Sarah running and fetching for them. All except Reggie, the engineer. Though he said nothing to her at first, he thought she was acting like a patsy. He got his own lunch and took his own clothes to the cleaners. He watched the circles under her eyes get darker and darker. He saw her give up her lunch hour three or four days out of five. When he couldn't restrain himself anymore, he asked her if she were happy in her job. "It's a lot of work," she said. "More than I thought it would be. The only parts I don't like are the errands. I get so backed up doing their errands, I don't have the time or energy to do my own."

When Reggie asked her why she put up with it, she just stared at him as if he had spoken to her in some obscure Tibetan dialect. "I'm a secretary," she said. "My job is to do whatever they ask me to do. Besides, they are all very nice to me. They take good care of me at raise time, and they let me go to any training programs I want to." Reggie didn't have the heart to remind her that it had been two years since she had had the time to attend a training program.

Eventually, of course, Sarah burned out. She saw that she was being taken advantage of. Her views switched completely. Instead of accepting everything her bosses gave her, she resented and resisted all her work, even the typing and taking of phone messages that any secretary would see as a normal part of the job.

What Sarah Johnson, Phil Gonzalez, and John Carr all failed to realize is that bosses are just human beings. That may seem pretty obvious to you, but I think all three of them suffered from similar misconceptions that the boss was automatically a god or a devil.

Why people have such severe problems with authority is a big question. Psychologists cite many possible reasons, all imbedded in childhood experiences. They call people who have trouble accepting authority of any kind "counterdependent." They say these are usually people who mistrust everyone, who are afraid of obligating themselves, who are driven to make a personal impact, or who have a cynical view of life.

HOW IT FEELS
TO HAVE PROBLEMS
WITH AUTHORITY

Power evokes strong but mixed emotions in people who resist authority. If you are one of these people, you will be drawn to and repelled by it at the same time. If you are a manager yourself you may be very good at managing others. Because you have such problems with power in others, you are probably sensitive enough to use your own power judiciously. You are also most likely very supportive of your people, helping them develop, going to bat for them if they need you.

If you fall into this category, you will find you react negatively to any pressure to conform. You dislike almost all rules and regulations. You may frequently hear yourself saying "red tape" or "stupid standard procedures." You may find it difficult if not impossible to control your temper when anyone pushes you to do something his way. You may see any criticism of you or your work, however mild or valid, as idiotic.

WHAT TO DO IF
THIS DESCRIBES YOU

If your feelings in this regard are extreme, you will have a hard time changing your basic attitudes. Many people find it nearly impossible to alter their fundamental response to authority, even with years of psychotherapy. But you can become aware of your feelings. With that self-knowledge, you can alter your behavior. You can understand what sets you off and control your response.

Look for a boss who will trust you and support you rather than one who will boss you around. Build your own credentials to elicit the kind of trust you need. If you have the right education, experience, or certification, they may let you make the rules, instead of imposing theirs on you.

Get yourself into an open, flexible company or industry rather than one that's rule-bound. Mavericks make out a lot better in product development than they do in banking. Look for work where you will not be closely supervised by anyone—sales, for instance. Start your own business. In other words, do what is the smart thing under any circumstances: Get a job that maximizes your strengths and minimizes your weaknesses.

15

DO-IT-YOURSELF MOTIVATION

*In order that people may be
happy in their work, these
three things are needed:
They must be fit for it.
They must not do too much
of it. And they must have
a sense of success in it.*

John Ruskin

I want you to figure something out. Get a piece of paper and a pencil. If, like many of us since the invention of calculators, you have forgotten how to add, subtract, and multiply, you may want to get a calculator, too. The math in this exercise will, however, be quite simple. Get what you need; I'll wait right here. Okay, here's what you need to do:

Write down the actual number of hours you are on the job each week, including overtime or the time you invest by arriving a few minutes early.

Now, figure out how much time it takes you to travel back and forth to work each day. Don't use the figure you tell your friends. Use the real number, including time spent in traffic jams. Multiply by five.

Calculate how much time you spend getting ready for work each morning and getting back into your home clothes each evening. Multiply by five.

If you bring work home with you, write down the number of hours you spend on homework each week.

If you are taking courses or working toward a degree that you hope will further your career, write down the number of hours you devote to that schooling each week. Include classroom time, study time, and commuting time to and from school.

Okay, now take the number of hours you sleep each night and multiply that by seven. Write down the result.

Add up all the figures.

Subtract this number from 168, the total number of hours in a week.

Your result is the total time you have left over each week. This is all you have to invest in buying and preparing and eating your food, maintaining your home, your car, your clothing, raising your children, visiting your mother, getting some exercise, making love, playing scrabble, balancing your checkbook, and reading this book. For the average person it's about fifty hours. It's not much.

No, I'm not trying to make you feel depressed. I merely want you to be realistic when you think about your career. If you are working full time, you are spending more of your waking life on the job than off. If you don't find some important satisfactions at work, you may not find them at all. If you abdicate your responsibility for what happens to you at work, you are giving someone else control of a significant portion of your time on this planet. If you decide that what happens at work is not your "real life," that what happens at home is what really counts, I can sympathize with your values. But you are effectively shortening your real life by about a third. It's time you started to take the part of your life you spend at work very seriously.

WHO'S IN CHARGE?

Motivation has always been seen as a management problem. It is and it isn't. It is, in the sense that managers can do many things, as we have discussed, to punch holes in people's motivation. On the other hand, if you allow your manager to take your motivation away from you, it is you who will have been robbed. And you can easily point to your boss as the cause, which indeed he may be. But you will have to be the cure.

You are in control of your life. George Giovannini learned this from one well-placed sentence. He was working as a staff assistant in the chairman's office at a major manufacturing company. It was a prestigious job, but he felt he was getting all the dumb assignments. He did his work enthusiastically at first, hoping that success in the easy projects would lead to more rewarding work. When his hopes didn't pan out, he decided to ask his boss, the staff vice president to the chairman of the board, why he didn't get better assignments. The talk got him exactly nowhere. The VP gave him several vague reasons, mostly having to do with his personality and the prejudices of managers in the company. Nothing improved.

For a month or so after that meeting, George ran on automatic pilot, doing the best job he could. Then the discouragement started to set in. He found that he had nothing to look forward to in his job. That depressed him. He thought about quitting, but he didn't. He excused himself for staying by citing the difficulties of getting another job. He told himself he couldn't move. He had to think of the kids' tuition, of the mortgage, of the explanations he would have to give his friends. He rationalized the whole thing. He never really allowed himself to consider leaving. He just went along feeling more and more trapped and getting more and more dejected about the work.

One day his colleague Earl walked by and saw George sitting in his office looking as sad as he'd ever seen another human being look. Earl just walked into George's office and sat down. "You look awful, George," he said. "What's wrong?"

"I feel like a bird in a cage," George answered.

Earl faced George squarely and said, "The door is open" and walked out. George sat there a few more minutes and went on with his work. Later on, though, he would trace the beginning of the changes in his life to that one sentence of Earl's. Those four words were enough to open a peephole to a better future. They rescued George from his own refusal to think about what was happening to him. They helped George realize he made the choices that determined his own present and future. It was his judgment about what mattered to him that governed what he did with his life. He decided to stop feeling like a victim. He found a job that challenged him. He took a temporary cut in pay to do it, but with his increased energy and enthusiasm, he soon made up for it. Now his life is better financially and psychologically than it ever would have been if he had stayed and let his motivation die.

Free will is a scary concept. It means you are in charge of your own motivation, in the driver's seat when it comes to your career. And it means setting your own destination and choosing your own route.

The choice of what to want or what to avoid is yours. The time calculations you did at the beginning of this chapter have convinced you, I hope, that you must get all the satisfaction you can from your work. But that does not mean you have to join the ulcer and coronary set, clambering up the organization chart. You don't have to become a manager just because society attaches greater prestige to that title. Climbing the corporate ladder is a rat race. Those of us who do it realize that. If you are ambitious, fine. But don't feel you have to choose what others say is best. It's hard enough to get the energy together to reach your own goals. I don't see how you could possibly keep striving toward career objectives someone else has imposed on you. If the rung you already occupy on the corporate ladder is comfortable for you, use the techniques we have been discussing to maximize the rewards and satisfactions you realize from your work.

In fact, many people have wrapped their personal definitions of happiness and self-worth too tightly with corporate success. I worry about people who plan their lives the way Bill Graves planned his. Bill was a trainee in an advertising agency. His head was full of "Yuppie" notions that other people had put there. The second time I met him, he told me this: "Well, I only plan to be with the agency about four years. As soon as I make account supervisor, I'll move over to the client side in a big marketing firm like Procter & Gamble or General Foods. After about four years in marketing, I'll be ready for a VP of marketing spot in a medium-sized company with a shot at the presidency by the time I'm forty-four."

He said that all in one breath, and he said "forty-four," not forty-five. I was appalled. I worried about what would happen to him if his plan didn't work out exactly the way he wanted. "What if you fall in love?" I asked.

He looked at me as if I had come down from Mars. "That won't matter," he said. "A family will be an asset to my career."

"But what if you fall in love with an idea, not a person?" I said. Bill wrinkled his brow and shook his head a little. He didn't understand my question. He didn't know a person could fall in love with an idea, even though he had already fallen in love with one himself. What will happen to him if the idea he loves betrays him? How will he cope with the disappointments that are bound to come?

LOGIC IS NOT THE ONLY WAY

Bill is trying to find personal success by following formulas. Life's not like that. In making your career choices, be careful of doing only the most logical things. The emotional satisfactions you derive from work are far more important to your motivation and therefore your ultimate success than any logical considerations. Sometimes, mistakes or wrong choices lead us to where we need to be.

For Margaret Caldwell, it was her emotions. After her divorce, several friends and relatives advised Margaret that the best way to support herself and her children was to take a job at the local savings bank. They had many logical reasons: she would have job security, good benefits, and a reliable albeit modest income. They wanted her to play it safe.

The trouble was that Margaret had always played it safe. Looking back, she wasn't impressed with the results. She wanted to become a new person. Over everyone's objections, she took a commission-only job as a sales representative. The only reason she could give for her choice was that she liked the idea of telling people she was in sales.

Her friends and family gave up trying to save Margaret from herself. They waited for her to fail and come to her senses. Meanwhile, Margaret was going about her job with gusto. She loved dressing up in her business suits. She felt glamorous taking customers to lunch. She kept a tally of her commissions in a little blue book. What she liked best was seeing that extra effort on her part meant more money for her and the kids. Her secret goal was to make more money than her husband had been making when he left her. It took a few years, but she did it. Eventually she was earning not just enough to support herself and her kids, but enough to take them on great vacations and buy them a larger house.

HOW TO MAKE CAREER CHOICES

Follow the heat and the light. Be sensible, but go to the thing that attracts you most. Strong feelings are often clues about needs that are buried deep within us. By following them, you may, as Margaret did, tap into reservoirs of energy and ambition you didn't know were there. If you deny your feelings you may be denying an underlying truth about yourself that will be there to haunt you and cause you to fail.

Stay flexible. If you can bend, you won't break. Remember, no matter how carefully you plan your career, no matter how confident you are, no matter how much energy you put into your work, life is still going to give you some surprises. This is a mystery story we are all living and what makes it interesting is that we don't know how it will turn out. Set your goals, but leave some room for the unexpected.

Remember, too, that if you don't realize your objective in one area, you will have other opportunities. The days of the single career path seem to be over. In fact, many experts feel that today's workers will have as many as five different careers. Change and risk and growth are bound to be a part of your work-life.

Learn to take criticism. Some people seem willing to do just about anything to avoid the disapproval of others, especially the criticism of someone in authority. To totally avoid the disapproval of others, you must give up your individuality. You must do only those things with which others will agree. Worse yet, you will eliminate any actions you think will displease them. If you do only what others expect, you will make yourself not only limited but boring.

Find a cheerleader, someone who believes in you and will encourage you to realize your potential. A friend, a parent, or a spouse can boost your ego, help you over the difficult times, keep you in perspective, and rejoice with you in your triumphs.

YOU CAN SURVIVE
CAREER MISTAKES

A number of different bad things can happen to you in your career. You could be fired or demoted, you could get stuck in a crummy job, or you could wind up working for a jerk corporation. When you suffer a setback, you will consciously or unconsciously choose to think the thoughts that will help you keep your sanity. Knowing how to cope with adversity is essential to your living a happy life. The best thing to do with it is to learn from it—about your work and especially about yourself. That learning will help your career. Besides, learning is one of two or three noble things you will do in your life. You might as well do as much of it as you can. Some people believe that it is the reason you are here in the first place.

Don't just up and quit. Today's workplace is increasingly regimented and automated. Rewarding work can be hard to find. You must be realistic in your expectations. If you have a stimulating job that has its faults, weigh the probabilities of finding something better before you give it up. Patience and cowardice are not the same thing. You may decide to hang in for a while instead of rushing ever forward. Ask yourself if things are likely to change if you practice a little tolerance. There may be other solutions besides going to another organization. Perhaps you can make some new contacts where you are; perhaps there are people around who will be receptive to your ideas; maybe you can create a different career path for yourself and stay where you are.

But remember that no decision is also a decision. If you decide not to go yet, you are deciding to stay at least for a while. Do it only if you have a chance of improving things. If the place is hopeless from your viewpoint, start looking right away. The faster you get out, the more of your energy and motivation you'll take with you when you go.

IF YOU DECIDE
TO CHANGE JOBS

Set yourself up to succeed. Take your time. Plan your move. Don't just escape to the first job that comes along. Use all the information that you have to find a job that will draw on your strengths and give you enough satisfaction to keep your motivation going.

Develop your skills. Go to training programs; take courses. If you can, put some energy into projects that will challenge you and help you educate yourself. These activities will broaden your choices and increase your chances of succeeding in the next job. The world is changing fast. You need the ability to learn and relearn. Those who refuse to adapt and retrain themselves condemn themselves to the ranks of the permanently unemployed.

Take a lateral move if it will get you out of a stifling atmosphere and if it offers you a renewed sense of challenge. Changing lanes may give you the space you need to move forward.

Expect some regrets. A job change is a complex, emotional step. You will feel ambivalence, a barely tolerable sentiment for many people. You will be happy to be making a new start, excited about the challenge, and energized by the sense of adventure. But you will also be afraid of failure, disoriented by the change in your daily routine, and sad to leave your friends. Understand that these feelings are all normal. For a period you will have to tolerate them. Try to prevent your anxiety from getting in the way of your success. Trust yourself to get used to the new schedule and procedures. Relationships that transcend work and have become real friendships will continue. As for the social ties at work, new ones with your new colleagues will soon replace them.

Let go of your anger. If you have been disappointed or frustrated with your experience at the job you are leaving, you may have developed considerable resentment. Leave it behind when you go. It will distract you from what you must do to succeed in your new place. Thoughts of revenge or bitterness will pollute your energy and personality. If you can't give them up, get help. Your new company will hire you for your skills, your experience, and the contribution you can make. You won't succeed if you are carrying a bag of negativity.

Part with your boss on cordial terms. Resist the temptation to make a dramatic exit. You've put up with a lot from your boss already; don't invite her revenge. If she or someone in the personnel department asks why you are leaving, by all means tell the truth. But say it in private and state it in terms of what you think or feel. Say "I need to feel my work is appreciated. I didn't feel that in this job." Or "I need a more stable environment. I think in my new job, priorities won't shift so often." This will allow your message to be heard. The alternatives are to make harsh accusations or to fib. Neither will be productive.

For instance, you can deliver your message in "you" or "he" terms. You can say, "You never said thank you or expressed any admiration for my contribution." Or "He is constantly changing priorities. I'm not sure he's mentally stable." If you take this approach you will tempt either the boss to counterattack or the personnel representative to conclude you are hostile. In either case an important message will not get through.

If you fib, as most people do, about reasons you're leaving, for sure the message will never get through. The jerks of this world will proceed unchecked. If we don't do anything to stop them, who will?

Invest your efforts, not your ego in your new job. Your sense of self-worth will be affected by your business successes and failures, but don't allow yourself to become emotionally dependent on whether the organization appreciates you. Organizations are not human beings. They aren't even dogs or cats. They cannot have emotions. If you expect them to repay your love or substitute for friends and family, you will be heading for a great disappointment. Loyalty means you should be doing the best job you can, not that you become emotionally dependent on an organization.

LOOK FOR FULFILLMENT
AWAY FROM THE JOB

We said earlier that speedy career progress will not always be possible. Getting ahead is an idea that seems to be embedded in the American consciousness. But we don't have to submit to life in the fast lane; we don't have to strive constantly. Becoming head of the department by your fortieth birthday isn't essential to living a satisfying life. If we all move too fast we all lose. What good is a lot of money if all it will buy you is shoddy goods or vacations in plastic resorts where the food is mediocre and the staff is rude?

In fact, the Peter Principle seems to be operating so well that it's hard to find anyone who does his job excellently anymore. Our clothing comes back from the cleaners still wrinkled and spotty; our mortgage payments don't get credited properly; our cars break down and rattle or need to be recalled. Maybe if we all stop trying to move up so fast we'll all be better at what we do. We'll get more job satisfaction from the work we do and better service from the people we do business with.

Work is central to our lives. It is a means of self-discovery and a vehicle for human development. But it is not the only means to these worthy ends. Family life, community service, crafts, sports, travel, and education are all ways we can satisfy our need for group membership, mental stimulation, and self-fulfillment. These satisfactions will become increasingly important over the near term because many of us will not achieve our overly optimistic career goals. In the long term, in post-industrial society, there will simply not be enough work to go around.

We are going to have to learn (and to teach our children, as well) to challenge ourselves in new ways. We have to learn to draw self-esteem from something besides pay increases. Otherwise, what will we do with our disappointment if we don't move up as fast as we would like? Lots of us try drugs and alcohol but without much success. They deaden the pain only until the intoxication wears off. Then we have to take another dose.

Some people are addicted to their careers. They are adrenaline junkies who need to feel stressed to feel alive. The exhaustion they create through overachievement is their sedative. We all need to take the time to smell, not only the flowers, but the pollution. We need to make our work as satisfying a part of our lives as we can, but we need to take the time to experience what is going on around us and to make our environments as benign as we can. We need to take responsibility for our own job satisfaction and motivation. We need to learn to demand better management and get it. But we also need to use these same strategies to arrange for safe, peaceful, and fulfilling lives for us and our children.

EPILOGUE

A CONFIDENTIAL NOTE TO BOSSES

*That leader is best whose
people say, when the work is done,
"We did it ourselves."*

Lao Tsu
Tao Teh Ching

You are probably reading this book for advice on what to do about your problems with your boss. But if you also supervise others, you may have found some of my comments stinging. Perhaps you feel I have been overly sympathetic with the employee and harsh in judging the boss. By now you know that I side with the underdog. But I'm a manager, too. And I spend a great deal of time with other managers in training sessions where we are all trying to get a handle on our profession. There are few universal truths and even fewer formulas that will help us get it right.

Management is hard work. It taxes us mentally and physically. That's why it pays more. That's why it accords us greater prestige in our communities and greater status within our organizations. If you are a middle manager you are pulled in several directions. You have the needs of your employees, the demands of your management, the cooperation and competition of your peers, and your own inner drives to deal with. I wouldn't blame you if you felt overtaxed.

On the other hand, the title manager and the perks that go with it imply that your primary focus must be the productivity and morale of the people who work for you. There are plenty of books, films, audio tapes, and training courses that will give you advice on how to do your job well. This is no place for me to go into detail about that. But I do have a few things I want to say to you.

Don't blame your boss for your failures as a manager, regardless of what a crazy, dim, or misguided SOB you happen to work for. Don't do it even in your own mind. And certainly don't do it to justify yourself to your employees. If your boss insists that you do things that are counterproductive, find the courage to resist. Use the techniques we've discussed in this book to manage your boss so that you can in turn manage your people. Feeling sorry for yourself and badmouthing your manager will make you appear weak and ineffectual. These traits will score you no points either with those above you or below you in the company.

Set an example for your people. I know that's an old-fashioned phrase, but it is still a powerful idea. Those who work for you will model their managerial behavior after yours. You can have the pleasure of shaping a whole generation of managers under you. If they, you, and the organization are going to prosper, you all have to use management techniques that pay off and that last. If you are truly dreadful at your job, your people may learn from you by negative example. It is possible to figure out how to do things right by watching someone else do them wrong. But there's no future for you in that approach.

Be yourself. Don't try to adopt a special "managerial personality." Be careful of authors and lecturers who tell you what kind of a person you must be to be a successful manager. Your best approach is to be natural and authentic. If you are annoyed but try to act as if nothing is bothering you, the dishonesty of your message will show through. You will confuse your people. They won't know what you want them to do or, worse yet, whether they can trust what you are saying. They will wind up guessing. And they will guess wrong.

If your personality doesn't lend itself to managing comfortably and easily, why are you in the job? If you don't have what it takes, you won't succeed. The increased pay and status will be short-lived and too dearly bought. Find another way to contribute. If you have personal problems that interfere with your managing well, find a way to solve them or you'll never enjoy your job and neither will anyone who reports to you.

Capitalize on your strengths. Another common wisdom. Managers' time is fragmented, and they often work at a frantic pace. You probably aren't paying enough attention to your own management skills. Take the time to figure out which of your managerial practices pay off and which don't. Keep a log of actions you try and how they pan out. Do it for a month or two and see which behaviors you should continue and which you should drop from your repertoire.

Control the work, not the people. Remember, your job is to get the work done, not to be a puppeteer who dictates everyone's precise actions. Your people will do their jobs willingly if they see their needs as people are satisfied in the doing. Find out what they want from the job and arrange for them to get as much of it as you can. In such circumstances they will do more than you would have the nerve to demand. Allow them to be themselves and bring out the best in them. Don't try to impose personality and character traits on them. It won't work any better with them than it does when you try to do that to yourself.

Concentrate on your job. I mean on managing the work of your group. Don't spend all of your time politicking or trying to impress top management. Focus on the product or service of your department. Improve it, produce it more efficiently, enlist the help of your subordinates in perfecting it. And learn to have fun while you're doing it.

Be careful who you agree to work for. Never work for a jerk; it may be catching.

INDEX